Close Calls and Foolhardy Romances:

The Maturation of an Environmentalist

Bruce Calhoun

LOST≋
COAST
PRESS
Fort Bragg,
California

Close Calls and Foolhardy Romances:
The Maturation of an Environmentalist

Copyright © 1999 Bruce Calhoun

Lost Coast Press
155 Cypress Street
Fort Bragg, Ca 95437

phone: 800-773-7782
fax: 707-964-7531
www.cypresshouse.com

Cover design by
Gopa Illustration & Design

ISBN: 1-88289741-2

Library of Congress Catalog Card No.: 99-73595

First Edition

Printed in the United States of America on recycled paper
by Data Reproductions Corp. of Rochester Hills, Michigan

This book is dedicated to all the educators
and students who have championed the
cause of rainforest conservation.

Acknowledgement

I wish to thank Kimberly Alexis Smith for making me want to write this book, and for editing it with such keen insight.

Contents

Rose 1

Act of Bravery 5

Gale 9

Slim 13

Nancy One 21

Alaska 29

Rambler 37

Nancy Two 41

Skagway 51

One Hundred Roses 57

Limelight 65

Capsized 71

Cal 79

Lost Soul 89

My Gift to Greg 95

Depression.. 107

That's Not a Knife 115

Dodgeville 123

Bionic Bruce 131

The Sinister Minister? 143

Roxanne 149

SAVE THE RAINFOREST, INC. 157

Happy Birthday 165

Salt of the Earth 183

Bilsa 197

Postscript 217

El Junque, Puerto Rico

CHAPTER ONE

ROSE

In 1800 there were 7.1 billion acres of rainforest.
Today only 3.5 billion acres remain.
— 1998–99 World Resources:
A Guide to the Global Environment

My mother was born in a log cabin in 1921, along the Jump River in northern Wisconsin, the third of five children, the second of three daughters. Her older sister was named Daisy, her younger sister Violet. Rose, Violet, Daisy.

I don't remember Violet. They say she was my favorite aunt, that I loved to be cradled in her arms. She shot herself in the head while I was still an infant.

Daisy was a red-haired spitfire, the first of the girls to leave home for the bright lights of the big city. Pretty and vivacious, she was soon living the glamorous life with the fast crowd in Chicago. The letters she wrote to my mother lured her down from Wisconsin.

My mother was pretty too, and had a lovely voice. For a while she sang in the swank nightclubs of Chicago and Milwaukee, and rubbed shoulders with gangster types. They used to take her into secret passages where she could spy the illegal gambling going on in secluded rooms.

This life was not without its dangers. A beautiful friend of hers from Milwaukee was almost kidnapped. At a Milwaukee club one night, two men tempted her with a singing contract and offered to take her to their Chicago studio in a cab then and there. She agreed, but wisely asked my mother and one of the band members to come along. The band member caught on to

1

these pimps when they offered the girls some drugs. He figured they were trying to dope them up so they could be used in Chicago's thriving sex trade. My mother, her friend, and the band member got out of the cab before it reached Milwaukee's city limits.

Another adventure didn't end so happily. This time my mother was working as a waitress in a bar in Chicago. It was her first job there. She was nineteen and awfully naive. The bartender took her under his wing, gave her advice and protected her from some of the undesirables who came in.

There was this one fellow who became a nuisance to my mother. He made a lot of crude comments to her and pinched her ass one night. That was enough for the bartender. He threw the guy out and told him to never come back.

The next night, however, the guy showed up with a gun. He shot the bartender. The bartender fell to his knees and, with blood pouring out his mouth, tried to ask for help. Mother, like everyone else in the bar, ignored his pleas and ran panic-stricken into one of the bathrooms. When she came back out the gunman was gone and the bartender lay dead on the barroom floor.

My mother's closest call may have come on a lonely night when she was walking home from work. She noticed a man following her. She hurried her pace, he hurried his pace. She turned the corner, he turned the corner. Then she began to run, and the race was on. As she neared her apartment she fumbled for her keys, knowing she would never have time to unlock the door and reach safety before the man caught up with her. She was right. As she was putting her key in the lock the man ran up and shoved her against the door. She turned around to face him. At that instant a car turning onto her street lit up the pair. He froze, and in a wink my mother unlocked her door and slipped inside.

Before she moved to Chicago, my mother worked at a roadhouse near Wisconsin Rapids. One of the other girls who worked at the roadhouse hated my mother because her brother had accidentally impaled his hand on my mother's ice pick as she was chipping ice on the bar. Mother tried to apologize, but it did no good. The girl was uncouth and naturally contrary. She nursed her grudge, and made mother's job as miserable as she could. One day as the two argued over something or other the girl threw a drink in my mother's face. The roadhouse owner saw that my mother's patience was at an end, and he said, "Get her, Rose."

A knockdown drag-out fight ensued. The girl was tough as leather, but my mother gave as good as she got. The kicking, biting, pinching, punching and hair pulling spilled out into the parking lot. The fight ended when the brother showed up. He didn't approve of his sister's behavior, and he dragged her off to his car, giving her a few wallops for fighting in public.

It was some time after this fight that a man named Orla stopped in at the roadhouse and met my mother. He asked her out, they dated, and eventually married and had two daughters, Nancy and Kathy. Their marriage did not work out. After the divorce and a few years of raising two girls on her own, my mother answered Dortha Calhoun's ad in the paper for a live-in housekeeper. Dortha's first wife had recently died, and he needed someone to take care of him and his adopted son, Donny. He hired my mother, and she, Nancy and Kathy moved into the big house on his farm not far from Madison. My sister Nancy loved living on the farm. She was a tomboy and delighted in playing with the farm animals. It was here, though, that she first fell — or was accidentally pushed by Donny — out the second-floor window of a house. She cracked her skull in this particular fall.

Nancy recovered, life went on, and soon my mother became pregnant. This precipitated a trip to Dubuque, Iowa, where my folks were married by a civil magistrate. I was born several months later. Five months later mother ended her second marriage and returned to the life of a single parent in Madison.

This is where I had my first adventure. I was lying in my crib, contentedly smiling up at the ceiling, when Mother came storming into the room and trundled me off to her old Ford. She drove us to the telephone company office, then went inside to berate the manager for the huge overcharge on her bill and demand its removal. The manager gave her some rigmarole about how he couldn't adjust the bill. She returned to her car in a rage, placed me in the front seat beside her and started the car. She jerked the shift stick into reverse and started backing up, jarring my door open. I fell out and rolled under the front wheel. My mother lunged after me, failed to grab me, and watched as the wheel began to press against my head. Then there was a thud. The car stalled. It had backed into a telephone pole.

CHAPTER TWO

ACT OF BRAVERY

"The forests and biological diversity of the tropics
are at the point of extinction, and heaven and earth
must be moved today. Tomorrow will be too late."
— Alvaro Ugalde, Conservationist

Time passed. Mother got work packing bacon at the Oscar Meyer plant, and met an amiable sergeant named Lucky from Truax Air Force Base. She saw Orla and Dortha at intervals, too. One time when my dad was visiting her, Orla stopped by unexpectedly. My poor dad got shoved into a closet until Orla departed. So went my mother's life.

Meanwhile my sisters and I were growing up without much supervision because my mother worked the night shift at Oscar Meyer. I wasn't much of a problem. It was the girls who were running wild. They were skipping school, shoplifting and breaking into Frito-Lay trucks. They'd use a crowbar to break into the trucks that were parked overnight in the company's lot, and then sit inside contentedly eating potato chips until they got sick.

They committed their most imaginative outrage against Mother. For some reason she had pissed them off. In retaliation they broke into her car at the plant parking lot, hot-wired it and parked it on the other side of the plant.

Soon after this stunt, Nancy fell out of a second story window in our upstairs apartment. This time she broke her back. She recovered, but this was the straw that broke the camel's back. For the good of the girls, Orla and mother decided to remarry.

Orla was the treasurer of Wisconsin's Ironworkers' Union. He was pretty well off so he was able to buy us a nice *one-story* house

5

in the country near Sun Prairie, a suburb of Madison. My sisters adjusted to living in the country quickly, but I was bored. I missed my city friends.

Gene Shep came to my rescue. He lived down the road in a huge old farmhouse with his folks and sister. He taught me his country ways. In the winter we'd go sledding down the hills on his farm. In the summer we'd bike to the pond to go fishing, gather berries in the fields and pick apples from the orchard. Every fall we'd go into the woods and collect the hickory nuts, walnuts and acorns his family needed to supplement their diet, Shep's family was poor and couldn't afford a lot of store-bought extras. We built a tree house in those woods, and cooked Oscar Meyer hams over an open fire. Gene really liked these hams because he didn't often get to eat his fill of meat.

I overstepped the boundaries of our friendship once when I stole a kiss from his sister. He got mad when he discovered us behind the woodpile. I didn't care, though. This had been my first kiss with a girl and I enjoyed the experience beyond measure.

Gene had other friends, the Peschels and Mike Mueller. I didn't like these kids. They were big and mean, and I was afraid of them. One day the Peschels, Mueller, Gene and I were playing in a gravel pit where a groundwater pond had formed. The Peschels had built a makeshift raft to navigate the pond. After a while they thought it would be fun to strand Mueller on a tiny islet out in the middle of the pond. Against his protests they transported him to the islet on their raft and dropped him off. Mueller just stood on his little island, and soon it became painfully obvious that this was a pretty dull game. The Peschels spiced things up by starting to throw rocks at Mueller, not intending to hit him but to splash up the water around him and get him wet. I stood and watched in dismay, thinking this could lead to no good. Then, as Mueller cursed at his tormentors, Gene joined in the rock throwing. Mueller and I were now the only ones not having fun.

It wasn't long before Mueller was soaked, and the charm of throwing rocks at him began to wear off. One of the bigger Peschels then said, "Okay Shep, it's your turn."

Gene was caught off-guard by this, and was unable to escape the clutches of two grinning Peschels. They dragged him onto the raft and started for the island. I didn't know what to do. Gene was my best friend, and though he probably deserved to receive the same treatment he had helped give Mueller, I couldn't stand by and see it happen. I yelled out to the Peschels to stop. They ignored me. I was a small and insignificant member of this outing, beneath the notice of these big boys.

The exchange took place. Mueller was taken off the islet and Gene was placed on it. When the raft returned to shore the stoning began. Gene begged for mercy. He screamed that he had new shoes on, that they had to last him for a year, and that they were ruining them. The Peschels laughed, and threw more stones.

Then the biggest Peschel had a brilliant idea. He got a large rock, put it on the raft and headed toward the islet. He was going to splash Gene really good. This I could not allow. With a pounding heart and a dread of consequences, I picked up the heaviest rock I could and hurled it at the raft. At the same time, Gene, in tears because his shoes had been ruined, began walking to shore through the neck-deep water, thus making my heroic act completely unnecessary.

The rock I threw fell far short of the raft with the biggest Peschel on it. It got everybody's attention, though, and raised the ire of the Peschel clan against me. The smallest of the Peschels was called upon to capture me for a trip to the islet. I was one step quicker. The only avenue of escape was a gravelly hill. I started scrambling up it. The little Peschel pursued me, egged on by his admiring older brothers and Mueller, whom I hadn't thrown a single stone at when he was on the islet. The little Peschel grabbed me by my feet and a cheer went up. For a moment I saw myself being pulled down the hill and rafted out to the island where I would meet the same terrible fate that Gene and Mueller had suffered. But not today.

I kicked the little Peschel hard in his jaw, and renewed my scramble up the hill. A little less enthusiastically now, the little Peschel chased me. Two more times he clutched at my feet. Two more times I kicked him. Then I was at the top of the hill, looking down at the little Peschel who was rubbing his jaw, and the other Peschels who were shaking their heads at the failure of the youngest member of their tribe. I had escaped!

Penas Blancas, First International Children's Rainforest, Costa Rica

CHAPTER THREE

GALE

Between 1960 and 1990, 1.1 billion acres of rainforest were destroyed. In the 1990s another 113 million acres were lost. Presently we are losing 64 acres every minute.
— The Last Frontiers Forest

A few years after the Pecshel incident my mother took me on a vacation to the lake country of Northern Wisconsin. Mother and I left Orla and the girls at home, drove to Rhinelander and co-rented a cabin with Barbara Braggers, a divorced woman who brought her son and two daughters. If there was one thing I liked as much as baseball, football and basketball, it was fishing, and the lake country was the place to do it. Barbara's son loved to fish too, but I soon learned he was a selfish brat, and avoided his company. Gale, on the other hand, was an angel. She was Barbara's youngest daughter, and about my age.

"So this is love," I thought.

Soon fishing was the last thing on my mind. I started spending as much time with Gale as I could. I took her boating on the small lake that bordered our cabin, and went for walks through the woods with her. Then I tried impressing her by turning over rocks along the lakeshore and catching the crayfish underneath.

I seemed to be making progress until we took a car ride to Copper Falls. My mother, Barbara and her boy Eliot were in the front seat. I was comfortably seated between Gale and her sister Cindy in the back seat. For the first half of the ride I was on cloud nine. The woods were beautiful, the skies were clear and the company was divine. As the road started to twist and turn, however, my little stomach became uneasy. I realized the grapes and summer sausage I'd had for breakfast were beginning to make me sick. I tried to think of something besides the motion of the car, the smell of the greasy potato chips Eliot was nosily eating, and the disgrace that would fall upon me if I were to get carsick.

"How far to Copper Falls?" I asked.

"Ten minutes," Mother said.

Ten minutes. It might as well have been ten hours. I looked around me. Was there a bag or something I could nonchalantly puke into? No. I looked into Gale's eyes. Would she understand it if the brave boy who fearlessly held monster crayfish in his hand suddenly upchucked in her lap? No. What was I to do? One more twist in the road, one more whiff of grease would do it. My guts contorted. My eyes swam. I clenched my fists. Mother took a curve. Eliot crunched on a potato chip. Gale pointed out a raccoon on the side of the road with its organs splattered all over the place. It was no use. I felt my stomach contract, and had no choice but to lean adroitly over Cindy and spew my ill-advised breakfast out the open window.

"Oh dear," mother said, "is my baby sick?"

She stopped the car and I was allowed out to complete the purging along the roadside. Eliot watched with glee, mother and Barbara with concern and Cindy with a degree of fascination. Gale on the other hand, demurely looked the other way so as not to witness my shame, though I'm sure she heard the gurgle and gush of it. When it was over we got back into the car and I was given a window seat. Ten minutes later we arrived at Copper Falls, where we all ended up having a wonderful time. Amid the splendor of the falls my motion sickness was largely forgotten, and to my vast relief I didn't give a repeat performance on the ride back to our cabin.

The cabin was situated on a wooded hill overlooking the lake. There were wooden stairs going down to a pier where we had a rowboat moored. Eliot couldn't swim so he was prohibited from going down to the lake without Cindy or one of the adults. This did not stop him. On several occasions he sneaked down to the pier to do some fishing on the sly. I happened to have been with him the last time that he did this. I told him he shouldn't be down here. He gave me some smart-ass remark and continued casting his lure out as far into the lake as he could. I watched him with dislike and wondered how it would feel to bury my fist in his abdomen. He edged closer to the end of the pier to make his next cast.

"Be careful," I warned.

"Mind your own business," he replied.

Eliot reeled in his line, looked at his lure, looked out at the lake, reached back as far as he could and whipped his fishing rod forward. His arm made a big arc and his body tipped forward. For one awkward moment he stood frozen on his toes, slightly inclined over the water. A second later he splashed into the water.

"This is great," I thought.

I ran to the edge of the pier and reached my hand out to him. He didn't even try to grab it. He just floundered around in a panic screaming for help. It dawned on me that this could be serious. I stretched out farther without being able to reach him. There was only one thing left to do: I took a few steps back and got a running start for my jump into the water to save Eliot. While in midair it occurred to me that it might be a good idea to summon some assistance. I yelled for help at the top of my lungs.

The moment I hit the water, Eliot was all over me. It was like being attacked by an octopus. My feet touched the bottom of the lake as I struggled with him, and it seemed the best thing to do was raise him up on my shoulders. This accomplished, his panic subsided. The situation was far from satisfactory, however. The depth of the water was such that Eliot could sit comfortably on my shoulders while I, on the other hand, was up to my forehead in the lake, looking quite silly, and unable to breath. This didn't seem to bother Eliot in the slightest. He made no effort to do anything. After holding my breath for a period of time, I determined on bending my knees and attempting a vertical jump. This worked just well enough to gain me a couple of gulps of air. After that I sank deeper into the muddy bottom of the lake where my jumping became futile.

"What do I do now?" I asked myself. "Am I going to stand here with this idiot on my shoulders until I drown, or am I going to try to dislodge him and make my own way to shore?"

Before I had to make up my mind I heard some yelling, then the sound of running feet on the pier. It was Cindy! She had heard my call for help. Calmly she laid hold of an oar on the pier and reached it out to us — a course of action I had curiously overlooked when I had been in her position. It was too late for that, though. We had worked our way too far out, so Cindy dove into the water. She removed Eliot from my shoulders and towed him to the pier where my mother, Barbara, and Gale had just arrived. I floated to the surface spitting up water. After pushing Eliot up onto the pier Cindy returned to help me.

As far as I was concerned this was when things really got bad. Both Barbara and my mother were hysterical, and when I got onto the pier my mother clutched me to her bosom, blubbering all over me. This was an embarrassment beyond bearing. As mom profusely thanked Cindy for saving my life, I felt that my humiliation was complete and my manhood completely undermined. Better to have drowned a thousand times than endure this, I mused, and abandoned all hope of ever winning the favors of sweet Gale.

CHAPTER FOUR

SLIM

Tropical rainforests contain 70 percent of the world's plants and 90 percent of its insects.
— Deforestation: Tropical
Forests in Decline

Gene Shep and his family moved away, and the Ashes bought their farmhouse and fixed it up. Jeff Ash, the eldest boy and two years my senior, became my fast friend. Meanwhile Orla and mother were having their ups and downs. Things hit rock bottom when Orla caught a bus to Chicago for business and left his new Bonneville at home. My mother took the car and picked up Lucky, with whom she was still friends. They decided to head down to a suburb of Chicago to see Aunt Daisy. As luck would have it they passed Orla's bus on the way down, and he saw them. This caused a big uproar, and mother and I moved out of the house and into a small apartment in Sun Prairie. This lasted only a few weeks. Orla and my mother patched things up and our family were reunited.

Orla treated me very well. I was the son he never had. He had sired only daughters — my sisters and three daughters from another marriage — and I think it pleased him to have a boy he could do things with. He was, however, a very important and busy man, and didn't have much time to spend with me. The most thoughtful thing he ever did for me was give me a genuine NFL football that had been signed by practically every player on Vince Lombardi's World Champion Green Bay Packers. I was a Chicago Bears fan at the time. I said, "Gee, I wish you could have got me a football signed by the Bears."

13

The last time I ever saw him alive he flipped me my half-dollar allowance and told me I was a fine boy. I was watching TV and wasn't paying much attention. I grabbed up the money, and told him goodbye as he walked out the door on his way to the hospital for an operation that was much more serious than I was led to believe. Three days later he was dead.

A great number of people attended Orla's funeral: ironworkers, union officials, congressmen, friends and family. I was too young to appreciate the eulogy he was given and the high regard in which he was held. All I understood was I missed him; it hurt, it didn't seem real. Standing there in front of his casket I felt woeful and vulnerable. The man who had been my father for the past four years was gone, *gone*. A profound sadness weighed down my heart.

Then I felt a strong reassuring hand on my shoulder. It was my dad, Dortha. I was dumbfounded. I hadn't seen him since my mother had remarried Orla, and had long given up hope that he cared about me. All of a sudden, there he was, and something in his face told me he had never stopped loving me. I was immensely comforted by his presence.

After the funeral my dad took me to Rennebohm's for a chocolate malt. There he explained that he had thought it best to bow out of the picture once my mother remarried. He had wanted me to have a normal life and look upon Orla as a real father. He said he had missed me very much over the past four years, that things would be different now, and that he would be as much of a father to me as he could.

Dortha's family was originally from the Kickapoo Valley country of southwestern Wisconsin. Before Dortha's birth, his father had migrated to California to seek his fortune as a farmer. He bought some land that turned out to be worthless for growing crops. He promptly sold it and returned to Wisconsin to start a dry goods store. It was later learned that the land in California was good for something after all. The new owner discovered it had oil and became a millionaire.

After fathering nine children, seven of them boys, Dortha's dad died. His mother decided to sell the dry goods store and move to Stoughton, Wisconsin, a satellite town of Madison. There the boys matured and built a farming empire.

It wasn't easy at first. To earn cash they took any job they could find, including delivering coal to people's houses by handcart. When they had enough money they bought a farm.

Working the farm earned them enough to buy another, then another. Soon all the boys had their own farms, and during harvest seasons the seven men would rotate from one farm to the next until all the hay, or corn, or wheat was harvested. They still had time to look in on their mother, to whom they were devoted. When they found out she had a suitor they decided they didn't like the idea. They locked the poor man in the cellar of their mom's farmhouse. Someone eventually let him out but he never bothered my grandmother again.

The Calhoun boys were famous in Stoughton in the early 1930s because of the baseball team they started, the Cooksville Orioles. Uncle Frank was the first baseman. He could hit the ball a ton, and he made all the local girls swoon. An agent for the Chicago Cubs tried to sign him to a farm league contract but Frank just laughed at him and said he already had it all. My dad played second base with the slightly withered leg his childhood polio had given him. Uncle Lou was the catcher. Uncle Pearlie took third base and the rest of the Calhouns filled the outfield. A neighboring farmer took up shortstop, and Uncle Frank found a fireballing pitcher from the not-too-distant city of Beloit. His addition to the team made it damn near invincible.

The glory days had passed by the time I was born. Uncle Pearlie had hanged himself in the barn with baling wire, because he saw his banker's car coming up the road and thought the banker was coming to foreclose on his farm. The other uncles just got old.

I have vivid memories of my summer stays at the Stoughton farm, before my mother remarried Orla and dad stopped visiting me. There were many chores to be done, chief among them the milking of the dairy herd. Once that was done the real work began.

My stays coincided with the hay harvest, and after the milking and a hardy breakfast, Donny, dad, a couple of cousins and I headed to the fields. Donny would drive the tractor that pulled the baling machine and wagon, while dad would hook the bales of hay coming out of the baling chute and heave them on to the wagon's deck. I would help stack the hay bales. It was hot, scratchy work, interrupted by frequent stops to grease the machines, reload baling string, and fix broken parts. When the wagon was stacked precariously high with hay, it was unhooked from the baling machine and replaced with the empty wagon my cousins would bring back from their trip to the barn after depositing the previous load in the hayloft. This went on all day, with short breaks for chocolate bars and soda when we did the wagon swap. We were always racing against the next rainstorm, which would wet and spoil the mown, raked hay. At the end of the day came supper, then a bath that left the sudsy water in the tub filled with the bits of chaff and hay.

The beauty of the harvest is that it filled the hayloft with bales of hay that made great building blocks for imaginative boys. We built chambers and tunnels, created labyrinths, fashioned sailing ships, and erected castles complete with dungeons. When we got tired of that we would swing from one pile of hay bales to another on ropes we had tied to the rafters above. At night we'd capture the pigeons that roosted on the crossbeams, transfixing them in the glare of our flashlights. Sometimes a colony of bees would nest in the hay. This precipitated a one-sided war in which we would dump buckets of water in their hive, and then flail away with wet gunnysacks at the airborne bees. We took our casualties but the result was always the same — the extinction of the colony.

Life did not revolve entirely around hay. There was pig castration day, which required little more than a sharp razor blade and a sterilizing solution. There was the cultivating of corn. This consisted of my father leisurely steering his tractor/cultivator down the cornrows while I sat next to him on the wheel cover, inhaling the aroma of his Winston cigarettes and listening to him sing folk ballads and love songs. There was the county fair, with its rides, games and displays of red and green factory-fresh tractors, mowers, rakes, combines, manure wagons, baling machines, planters, cultivators and elevators. There was also playful wrestling on the living room rug with my dad when the day's work was done, and the tales of gargoyles and goblins that he would tell me as I fell asleep in bed with him.

I only got mad at him twice: once when he spanked me for leaving a gate open and letting the cows get out, and once when he blew the big game. The big game was the only time I ever saw him and my mother socializing. It was a baseball contest between the girls and the boys, pitting my mother, sisters, an aunt and two girl cousins against Donny, dad and me. The game took place in the yard in front of the farmhouse, under the shade of several stately spruces. We boys were badly outnumbered but I was sure we could vanquish a team of females. It started out well enough. I would get on base, Donny would hit a home run, and dad would sometimes get a single. The girls were pathetic, especially my little cousins. We were building up a good lead when dad started making errors and popping up. As our precious lead began to slip away I played harder and harder. It was no use. By the last inning we had fallen behind. We had two outs and father was up. If only he got on base, I knew I could get a hit and Donny would hit a homer and we'd win. I crossed my fingers. The first pitch came. Dad swung and missed.

"Strike one," called my sister Kathy from the mound.

"Come on dad," I encouraged.

Kathy underhanded him another pitch, a real sweet one right down the pipe. Dad swung.

"Strike two." He smiled to the girls and shook his head in bewilderment. I didn't buy it — he was intentionally letting the girls win. When the next pitch came I closed my eyes.

"Strike three," roared Kathy, triumphantly. I opened my eyes to see the girls jumping for joy at their victory. I boiled over with rage.

"You let them win, you let them win," I cried, and ran into the house, my pride broken. Mother followed me inside, and so did one of the pretty little cousins I had a crush on.

"Don't cry honey," my mother said. "We were just having fun."

"Yes," my cousin added, "and you play really good."

This did not console me very much, and I pouted the rest of the day, doing my best to ruin the only time my parents had gotten to spend together since their divorce.

By the time of Orla's funeral, Donny had left dad to join the Air Force, and dad had gone through a depression, sold his Stoughton farm, and bought a smaller one near Mt. Vernon, in a hilly area southwest of Madison. This was a sheep farm, and I thought it a very lonely place the first time I saw it. It wasn't as much work as the Stoughton farm, except during the February lambing season. Then you had to stay up all night, periodically checking the ewes to make sure they weren't having trouble giving birth. During a weekend stay my friend Jeff Ash and I were trusted with this responsibility. We lasted until about 2:00 A.M., falling asleep over our civil war board game at that late hour. Dad rebuked us for this. I think he'd anticipated our falling asleep, though, and had gotten up early himself to make sure the ewes were all right.

Jeff and I went to dad's farm for a longer visit that summer. We helped with the hay harvest, which was pretty scary on the steep slopes of this new farm. We also mended fences, fixed farm machinery, sheared sheep, and toted rocks out of a newly cleared field.

We were at an age ripe for this kind of work, as well as for being the victims of the numerous pranks my father loved to play on us. One day we drove to the feed store and father bet us a dollar we didn't know our way home. On the return trip he asked us which way to go at an intersection. We correctly told him to go left, but he went right and got us home by another route. We accused him of fraud, but he insisted we had been lost, and took the dollar we had wagered.

The next morning we were rudely awakened when dad carefully wrapped some chains around our ankles and yanked us out of bed. "Rise and shine boys," he laughed. "You've got to get up early in the morning on this farm."

Worse than this, he sneaked behind our back to eat all the chocolate-covered cherries we had kept chilled in the icebox for a special treat. This was outrageous behavior, but he was so merry and unapologetic about it that we couldn't be cross with him.

Our dander would get up though, when he instigated fights. With two of us we thought we had the advantage, but he often seemed to be holding a cigarette at such moments. He'd use it as a weapon when the combat began to turn against him, and would make his escape by threatening to burn our little eyeballs out with it.

A few times we caught him without his "Greek Fire." The twisting of toes, fingers and arms, the pulling of hair, the locking of legs around the torso were all practiced. Inevitably we would overcome him and he would cry "Uncle." We'd always relax our hold on him then, thinking we had won a legitimate victory. As soon as we did, however, he would renew the contest, saying he hadn't meant his cry. Before we knew it he'd roughly pin us to the floor and demand our surrender.

"That's not fair," we would say, indignantly.

His response was to laugh at our repeated gullibility. Then he'd twist our toes till we begged for mercy. I either inherited his love for playing such dirty tricks, or learned it from him during these episodes.

Things got serious the following winter. I was already feeling badly about losing my starting place on our middle school basketball team because I had missed three critical free throws in a row at the end of a game. Then I got a call that my dad had been in an awful car crash. Mother rushed me to the hospital. There I found my father in bed, just becoming conscious, all bandaged up, tubes running everywhere. Weakly, he took my hand.

"The other driver?" he mumbled.

The other driver hadn't received a scratch, and I told him so. This was a big relief to him.

Then he said, "You're going to have to take care of the farm until I get better."

I nodded.

Dad recovered, and a month later Donny's military service ended. Donny returned to live with dad. This lifted his spirits quite a bit for he dearly loved his adopted son. The only problem was that Donny didn't like farming. He despised it, in fact, and made it clear he had other plans. So when I visited, father would talk about how I would someday take over the farm.

This was the state of things when I entered high school, in the fall of 1967. I was sitting in study hall about a week after Thanksgiving, when my name was announced over the loudspeaker. I was told to come to the office, and informed there that my sister would be picking me up. When Nancy arrived I was confirmed in my suspicions that something terrible had happened. She didn't want to tell me but I was insistent.

"Your father is dead," she said.

"Dead?" I said to my sister. But I had just talked to him on the phone a week ago, explaining why I had to cancel our plans to spend Thanksgiving together. He couldn't be dead.

Dad's funeral took place on a cold, cloudy, November day, like the one Orla was buried on two years earlier. This time there was no strong, comforting hand placed on my shoulder, only a few friends, family and a desolate-looking Donny. Twenty-five years later Donny would tell me how dad had felt poorly on the morning he died, how despite this Donny had cajoled him into coming out to help him mend the corn crib. He would tell me how after working on the crib for a while dad had been convulsed with a heart attack, turned purple, and stopped breathing. He would relate to me how, in desperation, he had climbed down inside the crib where father lay prostrate on the corn, lifted him up with such strength that father seemed to weigh no more than a feather, and entreated him not to die.

No, there were just a few of us at this funeral, and there was little solace to be had. I looked down at my lifeless father knowing I would never be able to take over his farm, and bitterly regretting that I had so seldom called him dad as he had requested, rather than Slim, the nickname he went by.

CHAPTER FIVE

NANCY ONE

*The skin of the poison dart frog contains
enough toxins to kill fifty full-grown men.*
— Save the Rainforest fact sheet

Even before my dad died I had begun to adore my personable freshman biology teacher, Harold Woodrell. The first day of class I confessed my fascination with crayfish to him, and not long after this, Mr. Woodrell had me thirsting for knowledge about all forms of life. This thirst spilled over into my other classes, and by the end of the quarter I had been transformed from a "C" student to a straight "A" student. Crayfish remained the fulcrum of my interest, however, and I spent many a late afternoon that fall down at the creek behind our house, collecting specimens for my twenty-gallon aquarium, which also contained juvenile pan fish.

With my father's death and the onset of winter, these collecting trips ceased. I brooded as Christmas approached. Other things were going on that disturbed me. Nancy, unwed and pregnant, was living at home with mother and me, and wasn't too pleasant to be around. Mother had been dating Rick — a man whose bout with polio had left him lamer than my dad had been from his own — and beginning to spend most of her spare time with him. Jeff and I were no longer friends. He had neglected "our" crayfish in the cow tank the previous summer when I was at my dad's. The tank developed a leak and all the crayfish died. This resulted in a schism that only worsened when he took up with Roger, who was his own age and, like Jeff, had a driver's license and a part-time job busing tables at a restaurant.

On top of this I had quit playing basketball. I never really recovered from the missed free throws and being benched, and it had gotten very difficult to get a ride home after practice. So that was over. The only good things in my life were school and a new friendship I was developing with Mike Bink, whom I'd met in eighth grade.

Things deteriorated further when mother announced she was going to Superior, Wisconsin with Rick over Christmas to meet his family. A pall settled over me. I became grim and resigned. On the morning of Christmas Eve we opened our presents, none of which pleased me in the giving or receiving. Then my mother and Rick left. Now it was only Nancy and me, and neither of us was in any holiday mood.

In a mean-spirited act I transferred her pet-store fish out of my auxiliary five-gallon aquarium to make room for a gravid female crayfish. The container I transferred them into was inadequate. The fish leaped out, and my sister discovered their pitiful, dried-out corpses on Christmas morning. She erupted in anger, and next thing I knew she had gone and put her fist through my twenty-gallon aquarium. There was water pouring onto the carpet, aquatic creatures flopping around on the floor, and my sister screaming bloody murder in her pain and rage.

Quietly and resentfully I cleaned up the mess while Nancy retired from the scene. Afterwards I felt I had to get out of the house, but where could I go? Certainly not to visit Jeff, and no other place was within walking distance. I put on my jacket and headed out the door.

It was a bleak, overcast day. I walked down to the creek where Jeff and I had collected crayfish together in happier times. I looked back at the house where my miserable sister sat. I thought of my father in his silent coffin below six feet of cold ground, and wept. A crisis of the soul was upon me, and when the tears dried up I decided to cross the creek and penetrate the gray woods ahead of me.

I emerged from the other side of the woods into the stubble of an ugly-looking cornfield that was exposed to a raw wind. A large hawk circled above this field. Perhaps seeing this majestic creature was the turning point for me. I trudged on a little more enthusiastically, wondering what else I might see. The exercise

and fresh air did me good, and further into the big woods I witnessed a most extraordinary sight, a cat sitting in a huge twig nest
high in a tree. At least it looked like a cat. I could only see its head.
I would have to report this sighting to Mr. Woodrell, I thought to
myself.

When I did, I learned that what I had seen was a great horned
owl. Mr. Woodrell told me that the owls didn't build their own
nests, and weren't shy about moving into old hawk nests. He also
said that my owl would find a mate in January, and be raising
hatchlings by March.

So it was my fascination with crayfish and the Christmas Day
Massacre of 1967 introduced me to the natural world beyond
the creek. I started getting up before dawn every morning to
walk out and study the nest. Ringo, the family dog, gladly accompanied me. On the way to the nest we sometimes came upon
the tracks of an animal or the animal itself. There were raccoons
and foxes about, and during mild breaks in the weather, skunks
and opossums put in appearances. The deer carcass I discovered
shocked me at first, then became another study site.

The owl found a mate and had a family. I watched the hatchlings
grow, and collected the regurgitated pellets of fur and bones that
they so generously provided. By the end of the school year I was
a budding naturalist, sure of what I wanted to do with my life.

My reward for doing well in school that year was a fishing trip
to Canada with one of my mother's brothers, Uncle Wayne. He
was a master outdoorsman who never failed to bring home a
deer during hunting season or a string of fish when he wetted his
line. He had passed on his woodsman skills to his sons and was
now doing the same for me.

Our drive north terminated a little beyond Kenora, Quebec,
where we rented a cabin on a scenic lake with rocky shores and
a backdrop of black and white spruce. The fishing was good in
this lake, but better in the lake beyond, so we portaged our boat
into the second lake. Immediately we began catching nice-sized
walleyes and hungry northern pikes. By evening we'd caught
more fish than I'd ever seen at one time. This was paradise.

We settled into a daily routine: a breakfast of fish, a portage to
the second lake to catch fish, a lunch break where we cooked fish
over an open fire on shore, then catching more fish. We'd return

to the cabin to clean and store them in ice chests for Wayne's home freezer, eat a supper of fish, then enjoy a good night's sleep full of dreams about fish. If not for the fact that I didn't like fish, I would never have wanted to leave that place. Luckily there were enough candy bars and potato chips to keep me going, and I was having the time of my life.

On the second-to-last day I snagged my line in a bay overlooked by steep cliffs. I yanked and yanked. Finally it seemed to be working free. I reeled in my line a little.

"That's no snag," my uncle said, adding, to himself, "it's always the green ones that have the luck."

I had hooked a big one!

"Keep your line taunt," Wayne instructed. "Reel him in steady."

I did as he directed. My reel squeaked and the tip of my pole bent down to the water's surface. I'd gain some line, then lose some as the leviathan beneath us fought to maintain its depth. After twenty minutes I was beginning to win the contest, but my hands were cramping up from fatigue and I feared I might not have the skill to land this trophy. It was better to hand over the job to my uncle and let him finish it. I offered him the pole. He shook his head.

"I'm getting tired," I said. "I can't crank anymore."

"He's yours to land or lose," Wayne responded. "Don't give up now."

So I continued the struggle. It was fish against human, a creature from below trying with all its might to escape a creature from above, two antagonists at the opposite ends of a nylon filament, trying to force their wills upon each other. It was the instinct, fear, and anger of an animal that could not understand what was happening versus the determined efforts of a boy who was coming of age. It was life for the one, glory for the other.

At length I forced the magnificent fish, a three-foot northern pike, to the surface. He wasn't quite ready to give up, and he made one last desperate plunge for the depths as Wayne tried to scoop him up. The pike's effort, however, was to no avail. With aching arms I reeled him back to the boat and into Wayne's doomsday net.

"Eighteen pounds at least," congratulated Wayne as he lifted my defeated adversary into our boat. "Be careful of that mouth. It could take a finger off." Later, when we cleaned it, we cut a three-pound pike out of its stomach.

The remainder of that summer, as well as my sophomore year, was uneventful. I became close friends with Mike, worked with him as a carpenter's helper for his dad, and went camping with him in the woods behind my house. I took countless walks in the countryside with Ringo and Xerxes — a puppy I had rescued from the animal shelter — bought a 35mm camera and started doing wildlife photography, and made up with Jeff.

In my junior year I got my driver's license and inherited my mother's old Rambler. This was a plain little box of a car with no radio and no sex appeal. It was reliable, though, and it had spunk. Mike and I celebrated my license by driving into Madison to see the movie *Blue Water, White Death*, a documentary about an ocean voyage of scientific discovery and hair-raising adventure. After the movie I went on and on about how I yearned to have experiences like the people in the film.

Mike wanted adventure, too. He talked about how he would like to become a pilot. "I want to learn to fly more than anything," he said.

Spring came, and Senator Gaylord Nelson promoted the first "Earth Day." Nelson was from Wisconsin, and was following in the tradition of two other great Wisconsin environmentalists, John Muir and Aldo Leopold. His idea was to have a day each spring devoted to celebrating nature and calling for an end to the abuse mankind was heaping on her.

I took up his cause in my school and formed an Earth Day committee. We had a meeting to invite other interested students. Only a few came. One was Nancy Wheaton. I was speechless. I had been enamored with her for some time. She was pretty, athletic, friendly and vivacious. To top it off she worked at the Garden Drive Inn, the only place I'd go for hamburgers. She was a year older than I was, and I'd never dared talk to her — except to order a Gardenburger. Now she was at our meeting, offering her artistic services to the committee.

"Could you design a display for the hallway?" I stammered.

"Sure," she said, smiling. "I'd love to." I stared at her.

"What kind of display?" she asked.

"Ah, oh, maybe something on pollution or overpopulation," I suggested.

"Okay," she replied. "Can we get together and go over the details?" she added.

"Um, sure, yeah," I said, suavely.

"When?" she asked.

"Tomorrow night?" I managed to say, feeling light-headed.

"Great, I'll stop by your place after cheerleading practice. Where do you live?"

Hot Dog! The most beautiful and popular girl in the whole damn school cared about the environment and was coming over to my house to work on an Earth Day project with me. We were going to sit side by side and design a display that would inform our fellow students about the destruction mankind was wreaking on nature. I was going to quote startling statistics to her, give vivid accounts of fouled rivers and overflowing garbage dumps, and explain how DDT was causing the extinction of bald eagles. She was going to gasp and say, "I never realized it was that bad."

Then I was going to introduce her to the gentle and lovable Xerxes, and suggest we take him for a walk before it got dark. She was going to say yes, and during our walk I would pick spring wild flowers for her, show her the secret places I most treasured, and instill in her a greater appreciation of nature's boundless beauty.

It was all going to result in our getting married and saving the world together. Yes, at the tender age of sixteen I had found the woman I would love forever and the cause I was destined to champion. I slept fitfully that night.

My classes dragged on endlessly the next day. I saw Nancy in the hallway only once. She smiled and said, "See you tonight."

The last class of the day was P. E. I was feeling exuberant by then. I ran the quarter mile from the school to the soccer field in nothing flat, and had to wait for the rest of the boys to join me. When the soccer game started I was everywhere, running up and down the field with unbridled energy. Could the day be any fairer? Could life be any sweeter? Could my joy be contained within my breast? Was there anyone on the planet so happy as I?

The ball came my way. In my euphoria I sprang into the air sideways to give it a kick that would long be remembered. I missed the ball and came down at a funny angle on my left leg. There was a shattering sound, and I felt as if someone had hit my lower left leg from behind with a big, flat stone. I looked back angrily, but no one was there.

"What's going on?" I wondered.

A second later, Mr. Hanson, the P. E. teacher, was beside me, telling me to lay back.

"Oh Jeez," said one of the boys who'd gathered around.

"Get up to the school and call an ambulance," Mr. Hanson ordered him. Then, to me, "I'm going to straighten your leg, don't look."

When he did, the jagged broken bone retracted beneath the skin, and he was able to put his hand on my wound and stop the blood from spurting out of me like a fountain.

"Christ," another boy commented.

"Be quiet!" Mr. Hanson admonished.

"You're going to be all right, Bruce," he assured me.

"All right?" I thought. Was this going to make me late for my meeting with Nancy?

I told Mr. Hanson I had to be home by 4:30. "I don't think you'll make it," he said. How do you feel?"

"Not too bad. I really need to be home by 4:30."

Mr. Hanson looked me in the eyes. "You've broken your leg, son. It's a compound fracture and you need to go to the hospital."

It began to sink in. I was seriously injured. Soon I began to feel a lot of pain. Confused, I tried to think. I had to let Nancy know what had happened. I couldn't stand her up.

"Steve," I said to one of the boys I knew, "Nancy Wheaton is meeting me at my house at 4:30. Tell her I may be a little late, can you?"

Steve nodded. The searing pain of a broken lower leg that was aligned to the rest of my body at an unnatural ninety degrees took over after that. I rolled my head back and forth and pulled at the grass with my hands.

Someone in the crowd said, "Is he going to die?" Again Mr. Hanson hushed the boys.

Finally the ambulance came and rushed me to the hospital. My mother was waiting for me with a worried look on her face. She didn't blubber all over me and I was thankful for that. A nurse, in a somewhat cavalier manner, took me into the X-ray room and turned my leg every which way for the camera. It didn't seem to bother her that this caused me the most exquisite agony. Then I was knocked out and operated on.

When I came to I had a forty-five-pound plaster cast on my leg, and it was 9:30PM I asked for the phone and called Nancy. Yes, she had heard. Yes, we'd get together soon and do the display.

It never happened. I didn't get out of the hospital for nine days, and Earth Day took place before I made it back to school. Nancy had slipped through my fingers, and with her my dazzling vision of the future.

CHAPTER SIX

ALASKA

*In New Guinea, kangaroos have adapted to living in trees and filling
the niche of monkeys, who never colonized the tropical island.*
— Save the Rainforest fact sheet

My favorite uncle was Sharon. He was my uncle by his marriage to Violet. He became something of a recluse after his wife had killed herself and his two daughters had grown up. He was a tall, grizzled, thin man who'd been a jack of all trades and had led an interesting life. He lived in a large one-room frame shack in the Baraboo Hills, an hour from Madison. I would drive up to visit him, and roam in the forests near his home, listen to him play the mandolin he had fashioned with his own hands, and eat his homemade strawberry shortcake.

In the evenings after his concerts he would regale me with tall tales of his youth, and the waning days of the logging boom in northern Wisconsin. He told me about the lumberjacks who would cut down grove after grove of majestic white pine, taking only the meat of the trees, the thick lower trunks, leaving a good portion of the brushy tops to go to waste. He told me the wolf stories he'd heard in the lumber camps. In one particularly harsh winter, as the story goes, a cook was returning from a railway supply depot to his camp in a horse-drawn sleigh filled with sides of beef. A pack of wolves, starving due to the severity of winter, began shadowing him. As night set in they became bolder, harassing the horses, nipping at their heels and snapping at their haunches. The horses were terrified, the sleigh in danger of capsizing. The cook untied a side of beef and threw it overboard. The wolves fell upon it ravenously, leaving the cook to go his way.

Sharon's best story was about the cougar. He had moved out west during the depression with his new bride, Violet, to work on the Grand Coulee Dam. Housing was scarce so they took up residence in an old abandoned cabin at the end of a remote dirt road. There was a cougar in the neighborhood that considered this cabin to be within its territory. One night, Sharon heard it prowling around on the roof. He woke Violet and told her they had cat problems. Then the cougar fell through a rotten part of the roof, smack dab into the middle of the room. It snarled in surprise, and must have looked around wildly. It was pitch dark in the cabin, and no one could see a thing. Violet kept still and quiet. Sharon did the only thing he could do. He edged his way to the door and opened it. The starlight illuminating the doorway showed the cougar the way out and the cat bolted past Sharon in a flash. After that, Violet made Sharon secure them more civilized quarters.

Uncle Sharon worked on the Alaska Highway, too. This was during World War II, when the United States Army was worried about Japan invading Alaska, and wanted a road connecting the lower forty-eight states to the northern territory. I was enthralled by his description of the challenges the men faced. They had to build over bogs that could swallow bulldozers, and bridge deep mountain gorges. They encountered bears, suffered unrelenting mosquito attacks in summer, and the frigid cold of winter that tested both men and machines to the limit. I was also enthralled with Jack London's *Call of the Wild* and I decided I would attend the University of Alaska — not exactly the news my doting mother wanted to hear.

"So far away," she gently chided.

"Mother, I'm going," I replied.

So it was in August 1971, mother and Rick drove me to O'Hare to catch my flight to Fairbanks via Seattle. Mother was melancholy. I was excited, but a little sad too. I rather doubted I'd ever want to return from Alaska. Perhaps I was hugging my mother goodbye for the last time.

Fairbanks was an isolated community of thirty thousand people, located in the heart of Alaska, and surrounded by forest, not far from the Arctic Circle. A railroad stretched four hundred miles south to Anchorage, and the Alcan Highway would presumably take you down to Canada and The States. The campus was just outside of town on a hill with a nice view of the Alaska Range and Mount McKinley, a hundred miles away.

The campus population was eclectic. There were Eskimos who had never left their native village before and were overwhelmed by the scale of Fairbanks and its mobs of people. There were Alaskans who'd grown up in the North Star State and considered the United States a foreign country. There were the oddballs, nonconformists and misfits who came up from the lower forty-eight, running away from something or simply looking for adventure. There were youngsters and retreads, students serious about an education, and students who were only along for the ride.

My roommate was Alaskan. He was from Delta Junction, a small town where the Alaska Highway turned southwest to Anchorage or southeast to Canada. He had run a trap-line at home, and had earned his tuition money by selling pelts of fox, wolverine and lynx. His wilderness experiences included being treed by an angry bull moose. We never became very close.

At campus orientation I met the two Kens. Ken from Massachusetts was Kennedy-like. He had bicycled all the way from the East Coast to be here, and had a heavy Boston accent. He wanted to be a mountain climber, so his friends christened him "Sir Hillary."

Ken from Rhode Island was his roommate. He was dubbed "Poseidon" because he was a scuba diver and had a long scraggly red beard. He carpeted their room with moss he'd gathered from the forest behind the dorm, and exhibited other eccentric behaviors that made him a personality worth knowing. The two Kens were also great Ping-Pong players.

I met Steve a few days later in the cafeteria, around which our social life centered. He was from Auburn, Washington, and had been lured to Fairbanks by romantic notions. He was taking some mining courses in preparation for prospecting for gold. His father had been a pilot for Trans-World Airlines and had flown the Alaskan route in the old four-prop Constellations. He had hooked Steve on Alaska with his ancient 8mm home movies of life in the sub-arctic. Steve and I rapidly became bosom buddies.

Steve introduced me to George, who was a Vietnam vet, a talented photographer and a former instructor for Outward

Bound. He taught me how to develop and mount my own color slides, and introduced me to Larry.

Larry was the patriarch of the cafeteria. He was in his forties, and working on a Ph.D. in education. He had taught school in just about every native village north of the Yukon, and had a knack for keeping a table full of people entertained with his jabber. He had a wife back home in California, but his titillating conversation attracted a buxom grad student in psychology who kept him warm through the long winter nights that were beginning to descend upon us. Larry introduced me to Eleanor.

Eleanor became my girlfriend. I soon learned that keeping a girlfriend on a campus where the ratio of men to women is three to one was not easy. My main competition came from an ugly and squat former Alaskan high school heavyweight wrestling champion who started hanging around our group.

One day I came out of the cafeteria to see him sitting with Eleanor on a couch in the lounge. She was laughing at something he had just said. "Do you want to go to the dance tonight?" he asked her right in front of me.

Eleanor looked up at me and said, "Sure, lets all go together."

"Count me out," I said.

A week later I organized a cranberry pick for the two Kens, Steve, Eleanor and me. Who should show up as we were about to depart but Greg, the wrestler? To my chagrin the rest of the party welcomed him. He gaily accompanied us into the spruce woods where the low bush cranberries abounded. I picked my quota of berries sullenly. When we had finished picking I began to lead us back to the dormitories.

"Wrong way," said Greg. "It's this way."

An argument followed in which Greg pointed out he was from Alaska and knew how to get around in the woods. I rebutted that I had scouted the area previously and knew exactly which direction we needed to go. My cranberry pickers stuck with me, and we made it back to the dorms in ten minutes.

This kind of stuff went on for a few weeks, and the dislike I felt for my rival intensified. I was wasting all my time fending him off while I should have been concentrating on Eleanor. Steve was sympathetic to my plight, and arranged a tryst for Eleanor and me in his room. We sat on Steve's bed and began kissing. She lay down, pulling me on top of her. The kissing became more serious, and Eleanor's body language strongly hinted that more was expected of me than kisses. I was not quite prepared for this, and I paused, not knowing what to do or say next.

"What's the matter?" Eleanor queried.

"Nothing," I said.

We kissed some more, and I stopped again, feeling very uncomfortable. I looked down at her and noticed for the first time that she bore a slight resemblance to my sister Kathy. That thought went directly to my tongue without passing through my brain.

"You know," I said, "you look like my sister."

The love light in her eyes went out instantly.

Eleanor dumped me and took up with an ex-sailor who had been waiting in the wings for her, someone who apparently knew what to do with a young girl as she writhed beneath him. Greg and I were both left out in the cold. With nothing else to do for recreation we often found ourselves in the Ping-Pong room together, learning the finer points of the game from the two Kens. I was more dexterous than Greg was, and when we played against each other I invariably beat him.

In cards it was different. He got his revenge by teaching me to play Cribbage, then trouncing me at it. Cribbage escalated to Pinochle, Pinochle to Bridge.

Ralph and Nils, the lounge-rats, taught us to play Bridge. Nils was the first Jewish person I had ever met. He was a case study in idiosyncrasy, and so uncoordinated that he couldn't eat a sandwich without dripping great quantities of mustard and mayonnaise all over himself. Ralph was a conceited, overweight Bridge aficionado.

Meanwhile Steve had hit pay dirt with Mary Brown. She and her friends, Alison and Denise, became part of our crowd. Denise was the prettiest of the three. She was out of bounds though, the fiancée of a boring engineering student from her hometown of Skagway, who promised to be a good provider. Alison was available — too available. She had the looks and demeanor of a matronly aunt. It was nice to have female company again, however, and the girls would usually give us their tickets on steak night so we could get double rations.

As time went on Greg and I began to lose our animosity to-

ward one another. Bridge was a team sport and we had to coop-
erate in order not to lose badly to Ralph and Nils. I began to
tolerate him to the extent of inviting him to my slide shows. He
grudgingly admitted his admiration for some of my pictures, and
I grew accustomed to the eyebrows that ran continuously across
his forehead, began to appreciate his sense of humor, and enjoy
the sound of his deep, lusty laugh. We cemented our friendship
over Thanksgiving on the train to Cantwell. I was going to spend
the holiday with Coop, a friend of George's, who was living with
his wife in a log cabin deep in the Alaska Range. Greg was continuing on to Anchorage to be with his family.

It was forty degrees below zero when the train pulled out of
the station in Fairbanks, and the oil stoves in the outdated passenger cars didn't provide much heat. To keep warm Greg proposed
we drink some of the blackberry brandy he had brought. I had
never touched alcohol in my life, but the brandy smelled sweet
and I was cold. I took a tentative sip. It was good, and it made my
throat and stomach glow. I took another sip, and so did Greg. We
looked out the window at the lonely landscape. It was two o'clock
in the afternoon and already getting dark. We started to talk, about
trivial things at first. The drunker we became, the darker it got
outside, the more our conversation waxed intimate.

It turned out Greg was from Wisconsin, too. When he was just
a tyke his parents had packed up their four boys and moved to
Alaska. His dad had signed on as a Federal Aviation Administration station manager. The first station his father managed had
been in Alaska's interior, where the family lived in complete isolation amid the splendor of birch and spruce forest. Greg remembered living on the second station, on an island in southeast Alaska,
better. Here the warm, wet climate encouraged the growth of
huge cedar and Sitka spruce, and the coastal waters teemed with
salmon, king crab and flounder. His father and a friend went out
into these waters to fish for flounder once too often and never
returned. Rescuers found their overturned boat and his father's
body. The friend's body was never recovered.

Greg took the last sip from the brandy bottle as the train pulled
into Cantwell. We looked out the window, only two log buildings, no people, no sign of activity.

"Are you going to be all right?" Greg asked.

"Sure," I said, drunk for the first time in my life. "Coop's meeting me."

I shook hands with my friend and got off the train. It disappeared into the premature night. I stood alone next to the tracks. An American flag flapped in the wind atop one of the buildings, a post office that was closed. I waited. The brandy flowing through my veins fortified me against the cold, and the novelty of my situation charmed me. Would Coop come? Had he gotten George's letter, or was the letter lying unopened in a post office somewhere? How much colder would it get? Was anyone else around? When would the next train come through?

Finally I heard some dogs barking. Soon, Coop and his wife came around a corner on their dogsled. They stopped beside me and we exchanged greetings, mine a little slurred. The brandy was having its full effect now.

"Ever drive a dogsled before?" Coop asked.

"Nope," I replied.

He threw my backpack on the sled. "Susan, show Bruce how to drive the team, I'll be right back." Coop started for the buildings and Susan beckoned me to the sled. I staggered over.

"Put your feet on the runners," she instructed. I did. She got on behind me and yelled, "Hi!"

The dogs took off so suddenly that my feet slipped from underneath me, causing both Susan and me to lose our footing on the runners. For a moment we both held on to the sled's handle and were dragged along. Then Susan lost her grip, and I was alone. I tried gaining my feet while maintaining a hold on the accelerating sled. That didn't work. Even sober I couldn't have done it. So I began running on my knees, enough to get one knee on a runner. The other knee was easy. I rose to my feet, and looked behind me. Susan was waving her arms and yelling. Then the dogs and sled and I turned the corner onto a trail.

We were in the forest now, racing along in the night, headed wherever it was the dogs had decided to go. In my stupor everything seemed surreal. The shadowy, stunted spruce looked like sentinels lining our path, with the occasional bough reaching out to slap me in the face and dust me with bitter crystals of snow. The Northern Lights, beginning to pulsate on the horizon, looked like a waving curtain of sparks. The dogs were like creatures possessed, running silently of their own volition, unaware of my existence. Mountains loomed ahead, all imposing, their cragged granite peaks resembling gargoyles in the reflected light of the Aurora Borealis. I stopped worrying about where I was going, and how mad Coop and Susan were going to be, and settled down to enjoy the ride. Half an hour later the dogs brought me to Coop's cabin, and stopped. I stumbled into the cabin and collapsed on their bed, where Coop and Susan found me hours later after their long walk home.

CHAPTER SEVEN

RAMBLER

Ecuador's tropical forests contain fifteen thousand plant species.
There are thirteen thousand plant species in all of Europe.
— The Primary Sources

Jeff had joined the army before I entered college. After his training he was stationed on Sheyma, the outermost island of the Aleutians in Alaska. Sheyma was a God-awfully desolate place to be deployed. The winds howled incessantly, the seas were furious, the cloud cover constant. No trees grew on Sheyma, no civilians ventured there. It was the most barren of military bases. Jeff was more than happy to get out of that place and visit me in Fairbanks when his leave came up.

I showed him around campus, took him to a party, got him drunk on cheap wine, and introduced him to my friends. Bells went off when he met Mary. These two were a match. Everyone saw that except poor Steve. By the time Jeff got on his plane to return to Sheyma it was obvious that Mary Brown was going to be Mrs. Jeff Ash someday.

Steve joined our bachelor's club after Jeff's visit. He started talking about quitting school to prospect gold, and we both recklessly considered buying an old C-46 cargo plane sitting out at the Fairbanks Airport, and ferrying it to Australia where we would start our own airline and become self-made men. This was during spring break, when everyone else had gone home to spend Easter with family.

With two days left before school recommenced I got an urge to go home for spring break myself. Steve loaned me the money for a plane ticket, and I flew on down to Madison. The purpose of my trip was to pick up my car, Rambler. To prepare for the thirty-five hundred mile drive to Fairbanks, I had her winterized and tuned, and acquired a half-dozen spare tires, two of them studded snow tires. Five days after returning to Wisconsin I was off again. If I drove hard I could be in Fairbanks in four days, and would only miss a week of classes.

The first day was easy. I had good weather and Interstate all the way. I made Minot, North Dakota by nightfall. That's when I hit the snow and two-way traffic. Just north of Minot I spun out of control in front of an approaching semi. I ended up in the ditch, and decided it was time to put on the big studded tires. They worked great. I slept that night in Canada.

Next day I started early and transited Regina, Calgary and Edmonton. That put me within striking distance of the Alcan Highway, and I kept driving into the night. By midnight I was cruising along the Alcan's snow-packed surface. Then I had a flat. Fortunately, this occurred a mile from the only motel gas station stop within sixty miles, and I was able to limp in without having to change the tire in darkness and sub-freezing temperatures. By seven the following morning I was on the road again, a thousand miles out from Fairbanks, putting mile after mile of forlorn country behind me. My goal was now to make the entire trip in three days, something I doubted a solo driver had ever done. Trusty Rambler would have to perform well to do this.

Midday found me passing through White Horse, with seven hundred long miles through nearly uninhabited country left to go. I stopped for gas, and had trouble starting Rambler again.

It was dark when I crossed the border into Alaska. I stopped for gas again, but didn't shut off the motor. It was idling rough. On I went, over paved road now. I was fatigued and almost fell asleep several times.

Then I got my second wind. I seemed super-alert, hypersensitive. I stopped one more time for gas in Delta Junction, and headed out on the last leg of the journey. Around 2:00 A.M. I started to feel tired again. Bleary-eyed, I noted milepost 75. I had an hour to go. In that last hour I noticed I was going downhill all the way, and had trouble keeping my speed below 80 mph. Finally I saw the lovely, welcoming lights of Fairbanks. I drove through town and onto campus, parking Rambler in front of my dorm. I got out of the car and could barely stand. I had been behind the wheel for twenty hours that day.

Rambler was a sad sight the next morning. She was filthy, her muffler was hanging down and she was listing over with a flat tire. She wouldn't start. Greg and Steve were impressed when I told them the details of my trip, but Greg corrected me about my descent into Fairbanks.

"The road doesn't go downhill into Fairbanks," he said. "It's flat level, you must have been delirious."

We resurrected Rambler. Greg tuned her up, Steve found an old Beluga horn for her that scared the Christ out of the cats we passed along the road, and I washed her and did a tire rotation. A cop stopped us on our way to get the muffler fixed, but we beat his ticket with some theatrics at the courthouse.

We did have a little mishap driving Ralph and Nils to a bridge tournament, though. There was a grinding noise that Greg insisted we should stop and check out. I told him I'd been hearing that noise for years. A couple of blocks later Rambler jolted and we skidded to a screeching halt as a tire rolled past us. I had not tightened the bolts on it enough.

Very few students had cars, and Rambler was popular on campus, but she passed into legend the night we went to Uncle Joe's for pizza. The school year was at an end and a group of us went there to celebrate. We ate pizza and drank beer till Joe's closed at 1:30 A.M. Once we were in the parking lot we discovered our group had swelled to ten people. We tried various combinations of loading the car. The best we could do was nine — Ralph, who could be counted as two people, Nils, and the two Kens crammed in back. Steve and Alison squeezed in tightly against me in front, and Preston and Mary sat on their laps. That still left Greg. I ruminated. What if I opened the trunk?

Rambler creaked and groaned as I eased her out onto the street, no give left in her springs and shocks. She handled like a tub, a ship too low in the water. Her tires rubbed on the frame when I turned; the slightest bump in the road caused her to sway. We must have been a strange sight driving gingerly down the street on that warm spring night in the dying twilight, front and back seats loaded and a large bearded man sitting in the open trunk. I'm sure the hitchhiker I stopped to pick up thought so.

"Get in," I said to him. He looked at me queerly. "There's room in the trunk."

The addition of this final passenger in the trunk caused Rambler's bow to tilt upward. But she faithfully took us back to campus, and later that summer, me back to Wisconsin.

CHAPTER EIGHT

NANCY TWO

Forty-three ant species were found in one tree in Peru —
the same number as are found in the British Isles.
— The Diversity of Life

My studies took a turn for the worse that first year in Fairbanks. My professors had proved uninspiring and my interest in a formal education had waned. I found my friends and the wide open spaces of Alaska much more appealing than the classroom. For a while I worked with a grad student who was studying hawk owls, and got some great pictures of the birds we snared with his traps. But when I wanted to do a photo spread for the *Fairbanks Times,* the grad student forbade me. He didn't want word to get out that research on hawk owls was being conducted until he'd concluded his work and gotten credit for breaking new ground in the study of raptorial behavior. This disillusioned me. In my idealism I had thought that scientific research was pure, the pursuit of knowledge noble and selfless. So academia lost its luster for me. I caroused with my friends, explored nature, took photographs and continued writing poetry.

When I returned to Wisconsin that summer I worked for Mike's dad again, saving my money to do something besides go to school. Mike was more on task. He had acquired a private pilot's license, and was planning to return to Racine to get his commercial and instrument ratings in the fall. He took me up and demonstrated his skills. To impress me he did some thirty-degree banks. I was so impressed that I threw up, filling my new red hat to the brim.

After a hot day's work on the construction site, Mike and I would drive back to the gravel pits behind my house to go for a cool swim. Sometimes there would be college girls from Madison skinny-dipping there, sometimes not. On weekends we would go to the disco bars, fruitlessly searching for women. At summer's end Mike returned to Racine to finish his pilot training. I flew off to San Francisco to catch a tramp freighter for Australia.

Finding a ship I could work passage to Australia on wasn't easy. On my first day of inquiry in the harbor office I was told I'd have to join a maritime union to get on a ship, and to do that I'd have to go to maritime school. I got a cheap room in a fleabag hotel down by the docks, and did some thinking. I wasn't about to give up, but it was clear that going through official channels wasn't going to work. The next day I searched the harbor for a rust bucket headed to Australia, with a Captain who didn't care about union contracts — a Captain from the old school who would shanghai a deck hand if he needed one. I didn't have any luck, and returned to my shabby hotel.

I visited the plush shipping offices downtown the following morning. Camera case in hand I told anyone who would listen to me that I was a photojournalist, and that I wanted to do a feature about the shipping line. This yielded me nothing, so it was back to the harbor, and an equally futile ship-by-ship canvas.

I became discouraged. I had been born into a modern age, I reflected. Everything was regulated now, free spirits were passé. There were rules to be obeyed, conventions to follow, formulas to slave by. Life was programmed, predictable. People were plugged into a system that made no allowances for individuality. They were on treadmills. No one was permitted to take chances anymore. The days of the adventurous vagabond were over, something you only read about, or saw in old Humphrey Bogart movies. Disconsolate, I walked back to the hotel. I entered the lobby and followed an absolutely stunning woman and her boyfriend into the dilapidated elevator. I wondered innocently to myself how the guy had wound up with such a hot number.

San Francisco is not the worst place to be shore-bound. After my morning ritual of scouring the docks for a tramp steamer, I would ride the trolleys, explore Chinatown, stroll through Fisherman's Wharf, visit city parks or travel out by bus to comb the beaches near the Golden Gate Bridge. In a week I'd become streetwise, too, awakening to the fact that prostitutes and petty thieves inhabited my part of town.

Just when I was about to give up on my dream of sailing across the Pacific to that land down under, I was told that an old Liberian freighter, the Cape Norte, had just docked, and that after she unloaded her cargo she would be departing for Australia. I went down to the harbor and found her. She didn't look so bad. I walked up the gangplank. No one stopped me. An officer on deck directed me to the Captain's office. I knocked on the door, and was greeted by a white-haired man with an olive complexion and a face etched by sea winds.

"Vhat do you vant?" he asked in broken English.

I explained. He rubbed his chin, looked at me hard, and told me he could use a cabin boy, that my duties would include serving meals in the officer's mess and cleaning latrines. I was ecstatic. Then he informed me that we would sail the next morning, and that he would need my passport and three hundred dollars to insure that I wouldn't jump ship in any port of call before we reached Australia. I wasn't so sure about this. Was the old dog trying to take advantage of me, cheat me out of money, and gain a power over me that would put me at his mercy? I hesitated.

"Do not vorry," he assured me. "Vhen ve reach Sydney you vill get your passport and money back."

I took him at his word and signed on. Early the next morning we sailed beneath the Golden Gate Bridge, and turned north to make the three-day trip to Tacoma and pick up the cargo we would take to Sydney via Honolulu. Happily I laid out the linen and plates of the officers mess. With satisfaction I washed the dirty dishes afterwards, scrubbed the heads, mopped floors, polished the brass on the bridge and did all the other menial tasks that were reserved for the person with the lowest status on a ship. I was taught my chores by John, the cabin boy I was replacing. John was an American who'd run out of luck and money in Australia, and could find no other way to get home but to work his passage. He'd flown to Australia thinking he had a position waiting for him as an engineer. The position was filled when he got there, so he worked at low-paying odd jobs while searching for employment that was more compatible with his education. Nothing came up and he left the country bitter. He told me Australia was a stink-hole, and that I was an idiot to spend thirty miserable days on this ship to go there.

The other cabin boy, Colin, was from England. He filled the niche of maid on the Cape Norte, and his opinion of Australia was the opposite of John's. Colin had arrived in Australia on a cruise ship, having partied his way across the ocean with a ship-load of debutantes and dandies. He had set foot on the island continent without a penny in his pocket or a thought to what he would do. For as long as his visa lasted he basked in the sunshine, making friends everywhere, playing the guest in beach houses, bathing nude in the sea with his Aussie girlfriends, and generally not giving a rip about the next day. He told me Australia was heaven. John scowled at this, and shook his head in contradiction.

John and Colin were the only human beings I conversed with on board. The crew was Portuguese, and the officers Yugoslavian. Neither group spoke English. The Captain spoke to me only on the rare occasions when he wanted something special done. I became concerned that the days would pass tediously once John and Colin debarked in Tacoma. I also began to feel the effects of the ocean swells. They nauseated me. Our cook's greasy food and the diesel fumes from Norte's great engine room exacerbated matters. I slept poorly my second night out.

The seas got rougher the third day, and by the time we made Tacoma I decided my sea roving days were over. I called Steve, who was living at home with his folks in Auburn, from a phone on the pier. He said he'd come pick me up, and I went to my cabin for my gear. As I packed I thought of all the trouble I'd gone through to find Cape Norte, and how after a three-day voyage I was saying goodbye to her.

"Life is funny," I said to myself. Then I went to the Captain in the slim hope that he would at least give me my passport. He listened to my explanation, and this rough-looking, ocean-chiseled man, who no doubt deeply loved the sea, nodded his head in understanding, not only giving me my passport, but also my three hundred dollars. It was good to be on land again, and with an old friend. It was early September, though, and I had decided that going to school was better than being seasick, so I hurried back to Wisconsin. When I got to the University of Wisconsin

Madison campus, I discovered I was too late to enroll in fall semester classes, so I got back on a plane and flew up to Fairbanks. They weren't so strict there, and I was welcomed with open arms despite being ten days late for classes.

Though some of the old crowd was still around, Greg had moved to Oakland to go to aviation school, and Denise had fulfilled her promise to marry her engineer, who took her back to Skagway to live. Steve was in Auburn, Larry had gone — with his Doctoral degree — back to his wife in California, and Preston had fallen into the rapids while fishing, and drowned. Things just weren't the same. Neither was I. I was the picture of discontentment until I met Nancy Smith.

Nancy was four years my senior, and the first time I saw her she was unloading a caribou off the roof of a car. She had just returned from the fall hunt with a male friend of hers, and was helping him with the animal he had shot and killed. I stood and watched them handle the caribou. When they set it down I asked her some question or other, which precipitated a conversation. Nancy told me she was from Washington, D.C., that she'd never been anywhere like Alaska before, and that the caribou hunt was wildly exciting.

"Washington, D.C.," I said. "What's it like to live there?"

"You can have D.C.," she said, dismissing the question, and we went on to talk about her caribou hunt. This led us to the subject of wolves. I told her about Coop's dog team, and the lead dog, Spitz, who was half wolf.

"I'd love to go dog-sledding," she said, and I knew she meant it. This girl reminded me of the heroine in Jack London's *Smoke Bellew*. She wanted to throw off the shackles of civilization. She wanted to experience nature in all its extremes, escape from her past and lose herself in the vast wilderness of an untamed land.

"Tell me more about Spitz," she said, ending my reverie. I did, and in so doing told her about the blizzard too.

The blizzard had been the climactic end to my Christmas stay at Coop's cabin the preceding winter. Coop and Susan wanted to go stateside for Christmas, and during my Thanksgiving visit they had asked me if I would watch their cabin and take care of the dogs while they were away. I gladly assented. It was agreed that I'd best not take the dogs sledding, but it was okay to take them for walks one or two at a time. Coop also warned me to look out for wolves. There was a pack in the vicinity and some distant neighbor's dogs had gone missing. Chained to stakes out of reach of each other, Coop's dogs would be easy prey for this pack if it came down the valley and found them unguarded. He left me his .22 caliber rifle.

The cabin became a lonely place after Coop and Susan left. I kept busy chopping wood, feeding dogs, breaking the ever-forming ice in the water hole on the nearby river, reading books and taking walks. But it was still lonely, even with the dogs for company. It was cold, too, and dark most of the time. Daylight was from 10:00 A.M. – 2:00 PM, and the mountains blocked any direct view of the sun. There wasn't much evidence of life around either. A few big ravens flew by once, their cawing and wing-beats breaking the icy silence, I spotted a snowshoe hare, and one night heard the booming call of a great gray owl. That was it until the night I heard a wolf begin howling across the river as I chopped wood by lantern light. This was the first time I had ever heard a wolf howl, but there was no mistaking it. It was a mournful sound that permeated the still, moonlit, snowy woods, that spoke to the soul of long-lost generations, that defined wildness and loneliness, and was so melancholy-sweet that it made your heart ache. I ceased chopping and listened for a long time, long enough for my body heat to dissipate and my toes to go rock-cold. Then I checked on the dogs. They were fine.

The next morning I ventured across the river with a couple of the dogs — and the rifle, just in case. I found the tracks; they were huge. I wondered how large a wolf could get, and where this particular wolf had gone, and where the rest of his pack was, and if they were experiencing a starvation winter like the pack that had chased the sleigh in my Uncle Sharon's story.

That night I waited to hear more howling. Nothing. I went to sleep. At about three in the morning I was wakened by a tremendous hubbub. I quickly lit the lantern, put on my parka and boots and grabbed the rifle. When I got to the dogs they were in a panic, whining, barking, and straining at their chains. I tried to reassure them, and held up the lantern as high as I could to illuminate the shadowy forest surrounding the kennel. I saw nothing, and after a while the dogs settled down. I stayed with them for the better part of a half-hour, then retired back into the cabin.

In the morning I checked the perimeter of the kennel. Sure enough there were wolf tracks around. The wolves had come within forty feet of the dogs. A shiver ran up my spine. This pack wanted to eat Coop's dogs. Had I not rushed out and scared them off with the lantern light they would have done it, too. Then I noticed that the sky was clouding over, and the wind was picking up. We were in for a howling blizzard.

It struck late in the day. The wind swept down from the mountaintops at gale force, whistling through the chinks between the cabin's log walls. When I went outside to check on the dogs, the snow was blowing in horizontal sheets, whitening the wind-ward side of the cabin, trees and dogs, who had curled themselves up into solemn balls. I went out to inspect the dogs again after supper. They seemed oblivious to the storm, and I supposed the wolf pack was hunkered down somewhere likewise, and wouldn't be prowling around on a night like this. Still, if the wolves did come it would be hard to hear the dogs barking in this wind, and I decided to sit up with my boots and parka on, and the lantern lit.

A few hours and another inspection later, I figured it was all right to catch a few winks. I dozed in the chair by the stove. I started, and half woke with a vague sense of *déjà vu*. Was I back on my father's farm, trying to stay awake on a cold February evening during lambing season? Was I letting my father down? Was a ewe out in the barn having trouble giving birth? I woke fully and noticed the wind had nearly stopped and the storm was abating. Uneasy, I took the rifle and lantern, and went out to check on the dogs. As I walked to the kennel the lantern began to flicker; it was running out of kerosene. In its dying light I saw the dogs were all sleeping, except for Spitz, the half-wolf lead-dog. He was sitting up, ears raised, hair standing along his back. The light went out. Spitz started to growl, waking up the other dogs, which commenced to whine. Then there was a snarling behind me. I turned but couldn't see anything. There was another snarl, some barking, more whining. I decided to run back to the cabin and fill the lantern with kerosene. In the darkness I tripped over a stump, and suddenly the dogs went wild. This was it, I thought.

Any second the wolves would pick their victim and attack, maybe Spitz, maybe in their confusion, me. I fired off several rounds from the rifle, and rose to my feet. I stood still for a while. The dogs quieted, the danger had passed.

Nancy gazed at me, eyes bright, and said, "Would you like to come to dinner tomorrow night?"

Nancy and I began to spend a lot of time together. She was easy to talk to and enthusiastic about everything Alaskan. She was enthusiastic about my poetry, too, which I had started reciting to her the day we took a long walk to an old abandoned farmstead called "Happy." It wasn't long before I was in love with her. Nancy was loath to talk about her past. I learned only that she had gone to a prep school in D.C. I wondered if she had come here to recover from a love affair, to forget about the man who had broken her heart. Or maybe she had become estranged from her rich father and had come to Alaska out of rebellion. I concluded, fancifully, that most likely she'd stumbled upon an important government secret and was in hiding. It didn't matter, the important thing was that she was here with me, and if she didn't want to talk about her past, I was more than willing to talk about mine — what there was of it.

Nancy lived in a grad student complex. Her apartment was the setting for our dinners together, and our wonderful talks about the many characters on campus and the many places in Alaska we both wanted to see. I lived up the hill from her in Bartlett Hall, with a new roommate, an Aleut from the Pribilof Islands, where the seal slaughter took place every summer. I didn't like my roommate. He was uncommunicative and morose, except when he had something to drink. Then he became rude and boisterous. Late one evening he and one of his buddies came back to the room intoxicated, with a drunken prostitute from Fairbanks' notorious Fourth Street. I pretended to sleep while they took turns with her.

Then I heard his friend say, "We should give your roommate a piece."

Their breath stank as they leaned over me, shaking my shoulders. I could feign sleep no longer, and exited the room with my bedding to repose in the lounge. Nancy's apartment was a sweet refuge from my unfortunate domestic situation.

Winter overtook autumn. I took Nancy to see the musk oxen, those stolid arctic ungulates that defied the cold with their long, shaggy hair and undercoating of cashmere, and made a gift to her of a short poem of mine that she liked more than any other. It was called *Holding Her*. It went like this:

Holding Her

Last fall before the snow had come
When in the wood my sweetheart holding
I took the time she used to laugh
To note the leaves
Were all —
So Golden

It was the only time she ever kissed me, and it was only on the cheek. After this high water mark I began to realize that Nancy was not in love with me. For a while I thought it was because I was too young. Then I thought it was because she loved somebody else, her friend the hunter, perhaps. I began to press, to knock on her door too often, or try to put my arm around her at a campus movie.

"Bruce," she finally told me, "I'm very fond of you, but I'm simply not capable of becoming involved with someone right now, can't we just be friends."

"No," I thought to myself, "we can't."

This was not the end, but it was the beginning of the end. By Christmas break I had turned as morose as my roommate, and decided to return to Wisconsin and continue my studies in Madison.

Two years later I read about a Dr. Smith in a newspaper article. He had practiced medicine in D. C. and had married a Kennedy. He had a daughter named Nancy. It all made sense now. Nancy was the niece of John F. Kennedy and his brother Bobby. She had come to Alaska to be healed, to lose herself in meeting people and exploring a novel world. She had come, I fathomed, to get away from the black clouds that hung over her family after the assassination of both her famous uncles. She had come to end the lamentation, to be swallowed up by landscapes indifferent to the tragic deaths of great men. She had come to Alaska to cleanse herself of sorrow, not to fall in love with me.

The author, holding a beetle from Costa Rica.

CHAPTER NINE

SKAGWAY

In the Upper Amazon, two-hundred and fifty different
tree species can be found in one hectare. Only forty
tree species exist in the entire state of Wisconsin.
— Save the Rainforest fact sheet

I changed my major from biology to English literature in Madison because, although I still loved nature, I hadn't found much satisfaction in the science courses I took in Alaska. The English department had some fine professors, and the one I drew for Introductory Shakespeare was a great teacher. He brought Shakespeare alive for the class, familiarizing us with Shakespeare's colloquialisms, describing life in sixteenth-century England, setting scenes in context for us and dramatizing the action with flair. He had us playing the roles of Hamlet, Othello, Desdemona, Falstaff and Prince Harry. He made us feel what it was like to be betrayed like King Lear, seduced into murder like Macbeth, or disappointed in love like Juliet. I could have listened to him soliloquize about Shakespeare ad infinitum, but summer came, school recessed, and I got a call from Jeff telling me that he and Mary were getting hitched in Skagway in June. I needed to get my butt up there to be his best man.

I didn't have the money for a plane ticket, and Rambler had seen better days, so I hitchhiked to Seattle with the aid of a brightly painted sign my sister Nancy made for me, and bought a cheap deck ticket on a ferry bound for Skagway. The passage north was pleasant except for the uncomfortable nights spent sleeping on lounge chairs. We sailed up the smooth-surfaced channels of Alaska's southeastern straits, passed shorelines resplendent with waterfalls, stopped in picturesque places like Ketchikan, where native totem poles still stood and the beautiful wooden fishing boats of the salmon fleet moored. Under low, moist clouds we witnessed the porpoise cavorting and bald eagles diving into the sea to catch fish. We saw a pod of Killer Whales, flocks of seabirds, and the glaciers of Juneau. When we reached Skagway Steve was there to meet me at the dock.

Steve had come up to Skagway at the invitation of Brownie, Mary's father, to work on the White Pass and Yukon Route, a narrow-gauge railroad connecting Skagway with the ore mines of Whitehorse. This suited Steve to a T. The railroad job paid well, and Skagway was the kind of place where a character like Steve could give free reign to his eccentricities. Still a frontier town of sorts, the streets were unpaved, the sidewalks made of wood. It was isolated from the influence of the outside world, and its year-round resident population was only seven hundred. Steve thrived there. With his newfound wealth he bought himself a cute little antique truck, in mint condition except for its missing doors. He also bought a small cruise boat, but ruined it by tying it securely to the floating dock's stationary pilings. When the tide came, in the dock rose but Steve's boat didn't, and the ocean flooded it.

When I say Steve was a character I mean it in every sense of the word. He did not look, talk, dress or act like a so-called normal person. He was short and spry. He had a luxuriant red beard and a pink nose. He always wore his trademark overalls, workboots and whatever unique hat he favored at the moment. He had a penchant for impractical, outdated things, and often told me he should have been born in the nineteenth century. He was a merry drinking companion and an accomplished honky-tonk piano player — two things that went hand in hand at the Skagway saloon where Steve was a celebrity. He was good-natured and fun to tease, becoming amusingly feisty if you played a practical joke on him — like stealing his macaroni and cheese or dumping a bucket of cold water on him while he was in the toilet stall.

The maddest he ever got at me was when I intentionally stretched Rambler too far as we were driving from Anchorage to Fairbanks on the newly completed gravel road. I had passed the last gas station for fifty miles with an empty tank just to get a rise out of him. He looked at the gas gauge as we drove by the station and told me I had better turn around. I smiled, patted the dashboard and said we'd make it. Steve didn't relish the idea of being stranded in the middle of nowhere. He tried to convince me I was being foolish, that we would never make it all the way to Cantwell without stopping for gas. I didn't turn around, however, and for the next half-hour Steve sat in his seat and fumed at my stubbornness.

At the halfway point I pulled over, saying, "Gee, I think you're right. We're not going to make it."

"I told you so," Steve exclaimed. "Why don't you ever listen to anyone? You're something else, you really are."

"Well, maybe you're right. It's too late now, though," I said. "Why don't you take over?"

We switched places and Steve drove us back on to the road. Behind the wheel he became more agitated. The gas gauge needle was resting below "empty," there wasn't any other traffic, and the road ahead promised nothing but more wilderness. As he drove he upbraided me for putting us in this predicament, ruefully telling me how easy it would have been to stop at the last gas station. I only nodded in agreement, noticing that Steve, in his anxiety, was driving faster and faster in a vain effort to reach the next station in time. Ten miles short of our goal Rambler sputtered and stalled. Steve got out of the car, slamming the door emphatically.

"Dag-nabbit, Bruce," he said. This was as profane as Steve ever got. "I'm not going for gas. You can go!"

I started walking, was picked up by a motorist, and returned with a can of gas to find Steve in a good mood over some nearby rocks he'd found that suggested to him there was gold in the area.

Steve took me directly from the Skagway dock to Brownie's house. Mary was there. She gave me a hug and introduced me to her father, mother and sister. I was taken in like part of the family, being the best man and the one who had introduced the fiancées. Steve was already at home there. Mary had never stopped liking him as a friend, and Brownie was immensely entertained by Steve's banter.

With me there, and Jeff scheduled to arrive in two weeks, excitement was in the air. But the first order of business was to find employment. I was broke, and would be unable to get back to

Wisconsin without help. There were no more railroad jobs to be had, so Brownie contracted with me to paint his house. My accommodations were already arranged; I was to live out at the tank farm with Steve.

We had a lot of good times in the two weeks before Jeff appeared. When work was done Steve and I often hiked up the mountain to Lower Lake. If we were feeling ambitious we went all the way to Upper Lake, a barren place above the tree line. Snow covered the rocky terrain around the lake until August. Steve thought the geology here was good for gold. He did a little prospecting, but came up empty.

The tidal flats were interesting to visit, also. They were gravel-bottomed, so when the tide was out we could drive Steve's truck around on them. One afternoon we took Barb and Bart out to the flats with us to have a party. Bart was the bartender at the Skagway Saloon. Barb was his girlfriend from Arizona. Steve parked his pride and joy a good distance from the water, and we all hopped in the back of the truck and made ourselves comfortable on an old couch we had brought along. Bart broke out some beer, and Steve began playing an old squeeze box he inherited from his grandfather. We all joined in Steve's rendition of "Springtime in Alaska," but for the most part Steve did the entertaining.

It wasn't long before the rest of us noticed the tide was coming in. With our eyes, we made an unspoken pact to play a little joke. Bart plied Steve with beer, Barb sidled next to him, requesting a special tune, I got up to stretch my legs, and blocked most of his view. The ocean crept our way, gradually eating up the flats as it inexorably approached the truck. The three of us could hardly contain our mirth when the water began flowing around the tires. We kept up the conspiracy a while longer, then Barb started to laugh. Steve looked at her quizzically, then looked inquiringly at me, which made me laugh. Then he saw what was happening and his jaw dropped. A hundred yards of sea was already between the shore and us. He must've thought his truck was already half-submerged, and about to meet the same fate as his boat. But the tidal slope here was gentle and the water only reached up to his hubcaps. When he saw this, his alarm subsided, and his temper, which we all so enjoyed seeing displayed, took over.

"Gol-dangit," he cussed, as vehemently as was possible for him.

"What the heck is wrong with you guys?" This was only the beginning of his harangue, which was why he was so comical when he got angry. He streamed admonitions as he climbed down into the cab of the truck: what did people think was so funny about things like this, and how would they like it if he pulled some hi-jinx on them, and what would be next after this?

We listened with glee, drinking up his righteous indignation. When he had trouble starting the truck, however, our amusement came to an abrupt end. Bart jumped down and quickly lifted the hood to fiddle with the carburetor. Steve tried it again. No luck. So Steve joined Bart under the hood, muttering to himself in such disgust that it would have been hilarious had the situation not been so dire.

After some tinkering Steve got back in the truck. It started this time and not a moment too soon. The water was up to the axle. As we drove to shore Steve rebuked us further for our prank, scolding us like a spinster aunt and shaking his head in wonder at our warped sense of humor, while we, relieved that no harm had been done, took our medicine.

Jeff was treated like royalty when he arrived. The Brown women fawned over him, and Brownie broke out his best liquor to celebrate. While Jeff was being pampered, and rehearsing for his nuptials, Steve and I prepared for his bachelor party, which took place at the tank farm the night before his wedding. We tried to get Barb to be our exotic dancer, but she declined, so as a substitute we pilfered a female store mannequin, dressed her in lingerie, and put her on the porch to greet our guests. Steve obtained a stag film for our edification, but one of the road gang workers stole it just before the festivities were about to begin. Brownie, who was a dispatcher for the White Pass, used his influence to get the film back, and the party was a smashing success. Everyone got roaring drunk, and Jeff was given his last rites.

In the morning I upchucked in the front yard of the farm — where I spent the night passed out after seeing off Jeff and Brownie — and got dressed. Still queasy, I rushed to the church and performed my duties as best man. Then I gobbled down some food at the reception, and returned to the tank farm for my gear. I met Jeff and Mary at the little airstrip Skagway boasted, and hitched a ride with them in the four-seated aircraft they had chartered to

Juneau. The ride was very rough, and I was afraid I was going to mar their wedding day by retching all over them. Thankfully the contents of my stomach remained where they were, and we landed without incident. The happy pair bid me a fond farewell, and sped off in a taxi to spend their wedding night in a comfortable hotel room. I, being short of cash and not too proud, found refuge underneath the bleachers of the softball field abutting Juneau Airport. By nine the following morning I had caught a flight to Seattle, where I found I was two bucks shy of the price of a plane ticket to Madison. The agent took pity on me, and made up the difference himself. I thanked him profusely, to which he replied, "You can buy me a cup of coffee next time you pass through."

CHAPTER TEN

ONE HUNDRED ROSES

*The fruit of the fig tree contains a laxative. This ensures
that the seeds of the fruit pass quickly through the
digestive tract of animals and are not damaged.*
— Save the Rainforest fact sheet

I made it back to Wisconsin in time for the pea harvest, and
landed a job driving a truck for Oconomowoc Canning. After
the pea fields were picked clean we started on the sweet corn,
which lasted till the fall term.

I moved into a dormitory on the shore of Lake Mendota, and
renewed my study of literature in an idyllic setting, reading clas-
sics like *Wuthering Heights, Tom Jones* and *Clarissa.* These were an
inspiration to me, and before long I had sought out and found a
sublime creature to adore. She was beautiful and exotic, the daughter of a diplomat, who had followed her distinguished father on
assignments to Asia and Africa. I had talked to her only once, over
dinner in our student commons, but worshiped her from afar.

Like any eighteenth-century lover I tortured myself over how
to win her heart. I racked my poor brain for a way to introduce
myself as a viable lover. Then I saw that a play was coming to
campus, an *avant-garde* musical based on *Romeo and Juliet.* I bought
two center-row tickets, placed one in an envelope with her name
on it, and slid it under her door.

This, I calculated with great satisfaction, would baffle and charm
her. "Where did this come from?" she would ask. "What is its
design?"

I imagined she would argue with herself as the night approached, thinking she would attend the performance to solve

the mystery, then deciding against it, then reconsidering. She would puzzle and speculate. She would scrutinize the faces in her classes and in the cafeteria, wondering who was the enigmatic stranger who had so boldly slipped his invitation beneath her door. She would hold the envelope in her lovely hand, examining it for a clue that might reveal the identity of its giver. She would bring it to her angelic nose and catch the scent of my cologne. She would talk to her friends, solicit their opinions, and then debate with herself some more. Finally, her curiosity would prove irresistible. She would put on her favorite outfit, walk to the theater and, with breathless anticipation, take her seat.

I was waiting nervously in an inconspicuous spot in the lobby when she arrived. She searched around with her eyes and proceeded into the theater hall. It was ten minutes before curtain, and I waited. I wanted to keep up the suspense as long as possible, then walk in suavely at the last moment, sit beside her and acknowledge with a casual nod of my head that, yes it was I, the handsome young man she had dined with a month ago, who was responsible. I was the intellect behind the scenario that had so intrigued her, and I who was to be her debonair companion for the night's events.

Just before the houselights went down I made my appearance. Was there disappointment in her eyes? I sat down. "So it's you," she said, crestfallen.

"Yes," I rejoined. "It's me."

An awkward silence followed.

"I can't quite remember your name."

"My name is Bruce Calhoun." At this point the theater darkened and the production commenced. The first scene convinced the entire audience that *Romeo and Juliet* was never meant to be set to music. She fidgeted in her seat. I whispered a witticism in her ear that seemed to have no effect. Between scenes I tried to arrest the deteriorating situation with a humorous observation pertaining to my socks. She smiled politely and turned her attention back to the horrible play.

By the end of the first act I realized it was hopeless. She had obviously kept our date in the expectation of meeting someone more "enigmatic" than I, and my lame attempts at being clever had even further disillusioned her with the evening. The complete failure of the performance was the *coup de grace*. When she excused herself to visit the ladies room, I knew she wouldn't be coming back. She avoided me like the plague the rest of the term.

Over Christmas break I weaseled out of my dormitory contract, and moved into a remodeled schoolhouse in the country with Rob, a rustic sort who'd picked me up in his battered old truck while I was hitchhiking into Madison. He established himself in the cozy basement. I took up residence in the drafty classroom above him. I put my bed in a little alcove and filled the classroom proper with a ghastly assortment of discarded furniture. When Chester moved in we built a freestanding wall that quartered off a corner of the classroom for him. My sister Nancy painted a mural on the wall, depicting Mike as a primitive cave man walking through a landscape dominated by volcanoes and populated by dinosaurs. Mike, who was living with his folks down the road, was not flattered by his likeness.

While living at the schoolhouse I formulated the plot of a novel for a group project in my Nineteenth-century Literature class. I outlined a dozen chapters and parceled out assignments to my group members. Our collective effort won us the plaudits of our professor. We all received A's at the end of the term.

I spent the ensuing summer driving truck for the cannery and writing stories that Rob, an editor for the *Wisconsin Department of Natural Resources* magazine, critiqued for me. When school started again I was more interested in becoming a world-traveled writer than a third-year literature major. I dropped out of the university in October and flew to Europe to see Jeff and Mary, who were stationed in Augsburg, Germany. My visit was an utter surprise to them. Mary was stunned and a little dismayed, having given birth to her first child only three days prior. Jeff took my sudden appearance in stride.

After a week with my friends I headed south by thumb and by rail into Yugoslavia and Italy. In Trieste I met two sisters who took me home to eat fresh oysters with their father, and to sample their mother's fine pasta. In Rome I marveled at the Coliseum.

I returned to Augsburg in late November. On my last evening there I went out for a beer or two. I had ten or twelve. When the owner of the pub closed his doors I caught the last tram to Jeff's.

But in my disoriented state I took the wrong tram and ended up on the opposite side of town. Entirely lost I wandered through the narrow streets in a cold, dreary drizzle, looking for a cab that I really couldn't afford.

"What am I doing here?" I thought. "What am I doing on this street? In this city? On this continent? Upon this earth?"

It grew foggy, it grew late. Not a soul was stirring in the streets. I alone haunted the night. Depressed and weary, I walked along until I turned a corner and came upon a cheerfully lit kiosk displaying a large poster of a beautiful woman. The woman's name was Mirie Matthieu, and the poster was an advertisement for her coming concert. She had exquisite eyes, jet-black hair and a smooth complexion. Her picture was set against a pink background that perfectly matched her inviting lips. As the kiosk light hummed and I stood there transfixed by her image, I could have sworn that she was looking back at me, that she was trying to part her soft lips to speak to me. My gloom lifted. The oppressive night turned sweet and liquid, the drizzle comforting, the fog friendly. I didn't welcome the cab that stopped to offer me a ride, but got in, took one last look back at the poster, and gave the driver Jeff's address.

Not long after I returned to the states Greg called me and proposed a winter tour of the American Southwest. It sounded good to me, so we decided to rendezvous in Seattle, where we planned to proceed, in his brother's car, down the coast to California.

I bought a badly dented Chevy for fifty dollars and set out from Wisconsin for Seattle. I made good time until I hit Idaho. There the car started to overheat. I stopped several times to put snow on the engine block to cool it off. This seemed to work. Then I realized the problem was just a bad indicator light. I drove on, increasing my speed to be on time to meet Greg's incoming flight from Hawaii.

When I got to Snoqualmie Pass, in western Washington, I was still behind schedule and it was beginning to snow. I stopped to gas up, picked up two hitchhikers who were thumbing at the station, and screeched out onto the highway. The road down the pass got worse, but I drove faster, and the hitchhikers grew concerned.

"Why are we going so fast?" one of them asked.

I explained the beauty of a perfect rendezvous, how a trip like the one Greg and I were taking had to begin on the proper note, how I had not seen Greg in two years and wanted to be there when he stepped off the plane. The hitchhikers didn't appreciate the urgency of the situation and became unnerved when the velocity of our descent down the slippery pass reached 80mph. They asked me to let them out. I replied that I had no time to stop. They must have thought I was a madman and disturbed me no further. They sat next to me — white as ghosts — until we reached the stop sign at the airport turnoff, where they hopped out of the car like jackrabbits. I arrived at SeaTac, parked my car, and ran to Greg's gate, meeting him just as he was deplaning.

Greg and I started down the coast after a brief visit with Steve and his folks, passing through Oregon and into California on the second day. Once in California we slowed our pace. It was cool and foggy, but we enjoyed the tide pools, quiet forests and empty campgrounds. Some days we traveled no more than forty miles. Eventually we reached San Francisco. Then it was on to Big Sur where we had a contest to see who could outlast the other diving into the ice-cold water of a river pool. We also had a singing competition to determine who could hold the last note of "Sixteen Tons" longest. Both contests ended in a draw. Disneyland and L. A. were next, then the zoo and Sea World in San Diego. After that we turned east to Tucson, and south to Mexico. From there we traveled on to visit Las Cruces, Carlsbad Caverns and Las Vegas. Then we drove west through Death Valley and finally north back to Seattle. In six weeks Greg and I had crisscrossed the Southwest and consolidated our friendship. We parted with plans to renew our travels the following winter.

When I returned from Seattle my mother asked me if I would drive up to Winnipeg, Canada with her. Why not, I thought. So again I was off. We followed the same route north that my Uncle Wayne had taken me on years ago, until we reached Kenora. Then we veered northwest, arriving in Winnipeg after a two-day drive.

My mother attended her convention and I knocked around the city. At the civic center I saw it — the Mirie Matthieu poster! I was stunned, and felt the same hypnotic attraction I had felt that autumn night in Augsburg. Her eyes were accented with long, fine lashes, her chin was round, her ear lobes small and delicate, and her lips were still pink, still soft and inviting. The poster was exactly the same as the one in Augsburg except for the text, which was an advertisement for the French singer's upcoming concert in two weeks. This was truly destiny. I looked around me, stealthily took down the poster, rolled it up and tenderly tucked it under my coat.

When I returned home to tell Chester, Mike, and Rob the electrifying news, only Chester got excited for me. Rob and Mike thought I was nuts, and couldn't believe I was planning to go all the way back to Winnipeg for the concert. Chester understood, though. He had a poet's heart and listened sympathetically as I explained how I was going to meet the French singer, win her love, and live with her happily ever after. He wished me God-speed as I climbed into my old Chevy to depart on my quest.

When I reached Winnipeg I checked into a cheap hotel. The next morning I went to the florist and ordered a hundred roses to be delivered to Mirie Matthieu at the Hotel Winnipeg, along with a note I had composed and had translated into French.

Late in the afternoon I went to Hotel Winnipeg, paying at the front desk to have the kitchen send a romantic dinner for two to Mirie's room. I waited in the service corridor for the bellhop to appear with the meal.

"Is that for Miss Matthieu?" I inquired when he rolled the cart into the corridor.

He looked at me suspiciously. I took out a ten-dollar bill and told him I had ordered the dinner and wanted to deliver it myself. He took the money, I took the cart.

"I'm going to need the room number," I said.

He put out his hand, I gave him another five dollars, and he furnished me the information.

I had no trouble finding her room. At her door I took a deep breath and knocked. My heart was beating like a drum, my knees were shaking, my whole being was aloft in the clouds. The door-knob turned and I came face to face with. with. a. large intimidating man with an ugly scar running down the length of his right cheek. For a moment I thought I had the wrong room, then I saw the roses and caught a glimpse of Mirie in a long, peach-colored nightgown. I opened my mouth to speak, but the body-guard pulled the cart into the room and slammed the door in my face before I had the chance.

It took me a while to recover from this unexpected setback, but I soon came up with another plan. As the time approached for her concert I stationed myself in the stairwell on her floor. I waited, peeking out of an inch wide crack in the door. An hour into my vigil the singer and her escort emerged from their room and walked toward the elevator. I hurried down the stairs to the next floor and pushed the "down" button of the elevator. A moment later the indicator light beamed and the door opened. There she was — the love of my life, the vision that had mesmerized me in Augsburg and summoned me to Winnipeg, the siren, Aphrodite, the mythical Helen of Troy whose face had launched a thousand ships. I stepped into the elevator. The door shut and we started our descent.

Mirie was staring blankly ahead, but her bodyguard recognized me and gave me a warning glare. I tried to step around him to talk to Mirie. He blocked my path. I tried his other side. He shifted to bar my way. I looked up at the floor indicator: 10, 9, 8. I was rapidly running out of time. I had only seconds to catch her attention and plead my case.

"Miss Matthieu," I shouted over the bodyguard's shoulder. She ignored me.

"Miss Matthieu." — 7, 6, 5 — the elevator was accelerating, speeding to the lobby where her fans would mob her and I would be lost in the crowd.

"Miss Matthieu," I cried again. "It's Bruce."

She pretended not to hear. "Bruce, I wrote you the note." At this point the bodyguard stepped into me, trying to push me away. I slid by him and confronted Mirie.

"The note," I said. "Did you get the note?"

"What note?" she asked.

"The note that came with the roses," I said.

Her lovely eyes brightened. "It was you? They are very beautiful."

The elevator came to a stop and its door opened to a lobby full of people. The bodyguard took Mirie by the arm and began guiding her through a sea of admirers. I ran alongside the singer.

"Did you get the note?" I asked.

"No," she replied, nodding this way and that to her fans.

I became separated from her, shoved my way past a few individuals and continued:

"In the note, in the note..."

We were swept outside the hotel, where a limousine waited with its door open.

"Merci beaucoup," she said to me, as she was ushered inside the limo. As it raced away I surmised what had happened to the note. The bodyguard had disposed of it before Mirie had a chance to read it. She didn't know anything about my infatuation with her.

I made a last attempt to see the singer at the civic center. I went backstage and tried to bribe the guard. He rebuffed me. I had no choice but to return to the theater hall and take my seat for the performance. Before it began two security men came for me. They removed me to the lobby and informed me that I would be kicked out of the place and worse if I caused any more trouble. I told them I understood, and was allowed to go back to my seat. After all, I now realized, who was I to woo an international star, a woman world famous for her skylark voice and incredible beauty, rich beyond my wildest expectations, sophisticated and doubtless pursued by men of real substance.

I sat teary-eyed, listening to her bittersweet songs of lost love, thinking that one of them, perhaps, was meant for me.

CHAPTER ELEVEN

LIMELIGHT

"We are living through the greatest age of
extinction since the dinosaurs died out."
— Juan Carlos Navarro, Conservationist

That spring Xerxes died of pneumonia. The vet couldn't cure him, and he released Xerxes to me in a near lifeless state. Xerxes' last night on earth was spent breathing shallowly as I lay beside him on the floor. I buried him the next morning, grief-stricken.

Xerxes had been my boon companion throughout high school. He had joyfully accompanied me on every walk I took in the backwoods. He had risen with me in the dark to trek to the fox den and see the kits emerge to frolic in the meadow at dawn. He had given me his evenings to walk in moon-shadowed woods. He had endured the wintry frosts and the deep snows I had so easily traveled over in my snowshoes. He had overcome his fear of water to swim across the gravel pit lake with me. He had stood by my side in respectful silence the day I discovered 'my' woods had been desecrated, and the tree that had held the owl's nest had been bulldozed down. When I had left for college he had neither understood nor complained. When hunters dognapped him, he had chewed through their rope and returned to my mother's house. When I came back from Alaska he was waiting, uncomplaining, ready to pick up where we'd left off. Then, at seven years of age, he succumbed to the virus that had almost killed me when I was a youngster. So ended his life story.

I began to read the Bible, not as believers do, finding comfort and meaning in their favorite passages, but as a scholar trying to

65

lose himself in his subject matter. By the time I had gotten to the New Testament, the pea season had started and I was back behind the wheel of a truck. Chester took a job driving a combine for the cannery, and the two of us suffered through a grueling month of eighteen and twenty-hour days. Throughout July our stamina was tested. We worked seven days a week. A full night's sleep was rare.

The corn came in August. Later that month Chester went back to school to finish his journalism degree. By then Steve had come to visit and stayed to drive truck with me. The cannery season ended in October, when the last of the red beets were dug out of the cool soil. Before that Steve had headed back up to Alaska, and I had decided I wasn't going to drive a truck for the rest of my life, that maybe it would be better to go back and study something more practical than literature. I applied at UW-La Crosse and was accepted into the biology program for the spring semester. This meant I had time after the beet harvest to join Greg on a diving trip to the Bahamas.

Greg had learned to scuba dive in Hawaii, and I had learned during the slow beet season. We drove to Miami in high spirits, arranged by phone for a twenty-dive package, and flew over to Nassau. Our dive-master, Bob, who also rented us the upstairs of his house on Paradise Island, was originally from Chicago. He had married an attractive Bahamian stewardess named Inez. We called him "Bad Bob" because he raised hell with his sleek speed-boat, smoked weed every night and trafficked in black coral.

During the day we dove with Bad Bob. In the evening I would go out on the town, and Greg, a natural born mechanic, would tinker with Bob's air compressor and fill our tanks for the next day. My outings alternated between the casino on Paradise Island and the cruise boats. Bob turned me on to a slot machine at the casino that would pay off twenty dollars every time if you followed the right procedure and didn't get greedy. This would supply me with enough money to go to a cruise boat the next night. Getting on board was tricky, though. You had to get someone on the cruise to bring you an extra boarding pass.

One night I tried it without a pass. I was explaining to the watch officer that my girlfriend worked as a bartender on the ship when a woman in a wheelchair, and her husband, showed up at the bottom of the ramp. The officer told me to wait, and descended to help the couple. Halfway down he looked back to make sure I was still waiting. I was. It wasn't until he was pushing the wheelchair up the ramp that I saluted him and dashed off into the ship.

He found me an hour later in one of the ship's bars and told me I had to get off the ship. I shrugged my shoulders in resignation and followed him out of the bar and down a hallway. He was careless, I let myself fall behind, and before he knew it I had slipped out through a side corridor.

I soon found myself in another bar. There were two very pretty girls at a table there. I went over, sat down and struck up a conversation. They told me, in their twanging accents, that they were from Alabama, and asked me how I was enjoying the cruise.

"Oh, I work on the boat," I told them. I went on to say I was the ship's detective, had caught a jewel thief on the last cruise, and that someone had once been mysteriously pushed overboard, and that another time I had broken up a smuggling ring. One of the girls ate this up like sugar. Before long we were slow-dancing and I was telling her how beautiful the harbor looked from Fort George, an abandoned structure on a nearby hill.

Her friend saw how things were going and discreetly excused herself, whereupon I plied my southern belle with another Piña Colada and asked if she wanted to catch a cab to the fort. She said yes. At that juncture the watch officer entered the bar through the main door. Unflustered, I raised Alabama by her hand and turned her toward the rear door, but there was a crewman standing there and another at a third door. As they converged on us the girl looked up at me questioningly. When they seized me under the arms she was flabbergasted, and must have thought she had been talking to some international master criminal.

They hauled me off the ship and the officer said that if he ever caught me doing this again he would throw me in the brig. I don't think cruise ships have a brig, though. I don't even know if they have ship's detectives.

When we had used up our twenty dives Greg and I packed our bags. Upon returning to Wisconsin I rented a house in the country outside La Crosse, and buckled down to study biology again. I got straight A's that semester, and spent a lot of time hiking the beautiful bluff country of La Crosse. I also learned to duel in a fencing class, and to appreciate classical music in Music Appreciation. I haven't picked up a foil since, but I still love to listen to Brahms, Saint-Saëns, Rimski-Korsakov, Mozart, Sibelius, Rachmaninoff, Vivaldi, Falla and Gustav Holst.

At semester's end I flew to Skagway, where Brownie had secured me a lucrative summer job as an engineer's assistant on the White Pass. I worked in the yard putting trains together, fueling and washing locomotives, and occasionally operating them. White Pass had rehired Steve as a conductor. We palled around together during our off time, often wading through the knee-deep Skagway River to explore a treeless gravel island that was home to an arctic tern colony. This always alarmed the nesting birds, which would dive at us with gusto, sometimes counting coup with a flick of their feet against our skulls.

In my wet suit, I also did some snorkeling around the piers. It was ice cold, but I was rewarded with a close look at the mussels, barnacles, urchins, crabs, starfish, anemones, shrimp, giant isopods, and kelp that made up the fantastic high-rise community clinging to the pilings. I was numb when I finished these dives, and people thought I was a little daft.

I confirmed their opinions when I quit my twenty-dollar an hour job in early August to meet Carol at the Calgary Stampede. She had debarked from a ferry one morning to do her laundry in town. When I first saw her in her boots, dirty sweater, baggy pants and baseball cap I thought she was a man. I was surprised to find out otherwise, and interested to learn that she'd been driving truck on the Alaska pipeline. When she took off her hat her long hair came down, and I noted she was actually a very nice-looking girl.

We carried on an animated conversation while she finished her wash, and I walked her back to the ferry. She waved goodbye to me from the bow as it was backing away from the dock, and shouted, "Come join me for Stampede."

Three days later I flew to Calgary, but failed to find Carol because she had never given me a definite address and the city proved too big for us to meet by chance. I finally gave up and returned to La Crosse.

The fall semester got off to a good start. I prepared some ex-

cellent diatom slides from the algae samples I brought back from
Skagway, and the house I was sharing with two roommates was
cheap. But these roommates turned out to be dull and messy, and
I fell out of favor with the biology department when I skipped a
weekend riverboat study trip to see Steve, who had been laid off
by White Pass and had come for a short visit. Consequently, I
began to spend more time in the fine arts building.

That's where I took my art requirement. I selected the erotic
art course, taught by a flamboyant and outrageous professor who
liked to paint penis-shaped clouds in his spare time. He was quite
proud of his creations, which I scoffed at during my frequent
stops at his studio retreat, where he entertained his students with
popcorn parties. Despite this, or because of it, Professor Kendrick
liked me. He said he wanted to do a portrait of my manhood. I
declined the honor, but did join his New York art student trip at
Thanksgiving. I got a D- in his course, though. He said I was
lucky to get that. As a joke I had "borrowed" his display, a sample
for our semester art project, and turned it in, poorly disguised, as
my own work.

During the second semester Professor Kendrick and I continued our association. He invited me to an exclusive party given by
one of his grad students. It took place in the student's artistically
decorated apartment. I arrived early and was treated to a tour
featuring mural photographs, modern sculpture, impractical furniture and a recessed hi-fi system. It was very impressive. Later,
when an attractive coed showed up I posed as the grad student.
There was no one around at the moment to contradict me, and
the girl didn't know our host personally.

The apartment really bowled her over, and I saw that she would
be putty in my hands if I could get her alone. The best way to do
this was to take her to my place, and right away, before she discovered my charade.

"Let's go over to my friend's house and get some more albums," I said to her, pretending boredom with the fabulous record
collection I was showing her.

"Why not?" she responded.

When we got to my house the door was locked. I took out my
key, winking at her and saying, "We're good friends, he has a key
to my apartment, too."

Inside she said, "Ugh, what a dump."

I rummaged through the fridge for a couple of beers and we sat down on the couch, ostensibly to look at some albums. I put my arm around her.

She said, "Let me go to the bathroom first."

I pointed the way. When she returned it was with a look of disgust on her face. "That bathroom is totally gross, let's go back to the party."

"In a minute," I said, coaxing her back onto the couch. A few minutes after that a roommate walked in, and I had to do some fancy footwork to get her out of there before my fraud was exposed. I was found out back at the party, however, when she met the real grad student.

When I told him the story, Kendrick tittered, "You rake. You cad. You bounder."

He said I had a proclivity for acting, and should try out for *Summer and Smoke,* a campus play. I did, but was saddled with being stage manager instead of getting a role. I watched the play from the wings and developed a crush on the leading lady. Her name was Bernadette, and I almost killed her and some other actors on our drive to the cast party when I raced in front of an onrushing locomotive at a crossing.

The next campus performance was a children's play, *Robin Hood.* I got the villain's part in this production. I was taught to joust, coached to be despicable and outfitted in thirteenth-century garb. I performed my part with such authenticity that the kids really did hate me, and booed every time I came on stage. I couldn't get enough of this.

After graduation the director offered me a job touring with his summer company. I almost took it, but I had already arranged to spend the summer in the Bahamas, diving with Bad Bob and writing a screenplay. I decided to stick with my plans.

CHAPTER TWELVE

CAPSIZED

*We lose a hundred species a day, four
species an hour, due to tropical deforestation.*
— Tropical Forests

I spent my first week in the Bahamas diving with Bob and living in a ramshackle guesthouse in Nassau's slums. The kitchen always had someone's prospective dinner of legless crabs turned upside down on the counter. The crabs' eyestalks would rotate eerily, as the unfortunate animals were still alive, and wondering, no doubt, what treatment they were to receive next. I don't think the crabs ever suspected they were to be boiled to make stew. The guesthouse also had a porch facing the filthy, busy street. There I worked on *Fidel Fidel,* the screenplay Joe wanted me to write.

I had met Joe at the campus pub during my final semester. He was the most handsome and charismatic man I'd ever seen, and was everything I wasn't. His eyes were dark and piercing, his jaw square, his smile irresistibly sexy. At the time he was living with a gorgeous woman in a quaint country cottage, and clerking at an adult bookstore. But this job was just temporary, an interim between his days as an almost rock star and his future as a famous director. He had taken some film courses at the university, and his family had connections in the movie industry in Mexico City. Upon mending his fences with his family and coming up with a script he would be on his way. This is where I came in. I had told him about some of my literary efforts, including a condensed version of the Bible that I had sent in to Reader's Digest. When he heard this he persuaded me that I could be a Hollywood screenwriter and told me he would work on a storyboard while I was writing the script in the Bahamas.

I was making some progress on the screenplay when Bad Bob suggested I catch a mail boat and see some more of the islands. I took his advice and booked passage on a vessel bound for the Exuma Islands. The boat carried more chickens, pigs, goats, produce and people than it did mail. It dropped me off at Staniel Key where I lodged at a small marina hotel and explored the surroundings.

The following day an extraordinary young man named Barry sailed into the harbor in a seventeen-foot boat he had navigated down the Florida coast, across the Gulf Stream and up from Andros Island. The little craft lacked a cabin and a deck, and its freeboard was a mere sixteen inches. The locals were amazed by Barry's feat of seamanship, and he became an island celebrity. I was the one who befriended the barefoot, tattered, lean and leather-brown sailor, though. I invited him to share my room, and for the first time in a month he slept in a soft bed with a roof over his head and no mosquitoes buzzing in his ear.

In return he took me out for a sail around Staniel Key. He gave me some turns on the tiller and said he was sorry he had already asked a Brit to sail with him to Eleuthera. But that impediment was removed when the Brit was tossed off Staniel Key for drunk and obscene behavior. Early the next morning Barry and I set sail across the tongue of the ocean toward Eleuthera, fifty miles distant.

Staniel Key receded slowly behind us as we took to deep water. We rode the swells gracefully, main and foresail spread to the wind, Barry standing legs astride and barefoot at the tiller. The water was deep purple and the sky a brilliant blue. But to our rear was a squall, a wall of gray rain that was engulfing Staniel Key. I asked Barry if it looked bad. He shook his head no. When the wind stiffened he gave me the tiller and stepped nimbly to the bow where he lowered the foresail.

The squall caught up with us, drove us hard into some waves, soaked us and passed. We bailed the water from the bottom of the boat and Barry raised the foresail again. I was at the tiller now, and began to enjoy the sensation of steering the vessel over an ocean that, with the addition of my weight in the boat, was only twelve inches from pouring over our side.

I guided the craft from a seated position, exhilarated by the power of the wind filling our sails and the energy of the sea we glided upon. I was barefoot too, and could feel the exuberance of the heaving ocean through the hull's thin planking. Precariously, it seemed to me, we would rise with a five-foot swell and dip back into a trough, each time daring the sea to swamp us. But we always avoided disaster by at least three or four inches, and soon I became accustomed, like Barry, to the nearness of the salty water.

At the top of a wave we often startled flying fish. They would jet out of the purple sea and lock their pectoral fins for the hundred-foot flight to safety. Sometimes we would scare up two or three at a time, and we marked our progress to Eleuthera by keeping count of them and noting the shrinking size of Staniel Key to our stern.

By noon another squall line had passed us and Staniel Key had completely disappeared below the horizon. There was no sight of land now, just the prospect of it, thirty-five miles to our northeast. Barry took back the tiller, and we had a lunch of raw conch salad, which I threw up an hour later.

"Are you all right?" Barry asked.

"A little seasick," I replied. "It's the motion and the conch salad."

"Take the tiller," he said. "It'll keep your mind off your stomach, and have a few crackers."

I did as he advised, taking the tiller, which was just an oar fastened to a stern oarlock, and munched on the dry crackers. I kept our compass bearing, breathed in the sea-fresh air, and half listened to Barry. He described in loving detail how he had built his boat at his home along the South Carolina coast. Then he told me how he had sailed down to Miami, endured the hardship of a twenty-hour crossing to Bimini, persevered through mosquito-infested nights in the Andros Bights and weathered a gale off New Providence.

It was late afternoon when the faint outline of Eleuthera slowly became discernible. Finally Barry said, "Uh huh, that's Eleuthera all right."

"Will we make landfall before dark?" I asked.

"Just after, I reckon."

That was good news. I didn't relish the thought of night sailing, and the sea was getting more boisterous. A third squall had hit us, requiring an alarming amount of bailing. Furthermore the swells were now six or seven feet. The winds were stronger too. Barry had permanently taken down the foresail.

When dusk arrived Eleuthera was in plain sight, her lights beginning to twinkle. I had gotten sick again, and relieved Barry at the helm once more in order to distract myself from my misery. He was watching the action of the boat more keenly now, observing, as was I, that some of the waves were coming perilously close to the top of our gunwales.

"We're loaded heavy for this kind of weather," he commented.

"Do you want to take the tiller?" I asked.

"No, you're doing fine."

I looked at him worriedly.

"I've been in worse that this," he reassured me.

I sailed us into the gathering darkness, wanting only to reach land now, disconcerted by the eager winds that were bringing another squall, and recalling Bad Bob's stories about people who had put out to sea in the Devil's Triangle and never been heard from again. We dipped into the bottom of an eight-foot swell that came within a sliver of flooding us.

"Give me my B.C.," I said. "It's in my duffel bag."

"We're okay," Barry replied.

"I want my B.C." He opened the duffel, pulled out my inflatable diving vest and handed it to me. I slipped it on. A moment later we dipped into another trough, too deeply this time, and with an awful, violent rush the ocean poured in over the starboard rail. We righted for a second. Barry began bailing frantically and yelled for me to bring her to port. I tried, realizing that our lives were suddenly in jeopardy. But the brave, tiny craft responded sluggishly. The next swell overwhelmed her stern, completely filling us with water and, with a final flourish, tipping us over.

Utter chaos followed. Barry and I were thrown into the water along with our personal belongings, some of which were buoyant and popped up around the capsized hull of our stricken vessel. I swam to the hull, blowing air into my vest. Barry tried to grab a nearby duffel bag that had resurfaced because it had a rubber wet suit in it. The ocean carried it out of his reach. Giving up his effort he grasped the hull and shouted for me to swim after the duffel.

"Why?" I shouted back, water slapping in my face.

"I'm going to strap it to the boat to make it more buoyant. We need the ice chests and life preservers too."

I looked around at the rapidly dispersing objects he was referring to. "Rope me off," I said.

"There's no time."

"I'm not going out there without a line," I insisted.

Barry groped in the water and found his anchor rope. He quickly tied it around my waist and I headed out to get the duffel. I retrieved it easily. Then I headed in another direction for one of the Styrofoam ice chests. I could barely see it in the darkness, and had to swim to the far side of a big swell to capture it. Barry and the boat were now out of sight, and I was glad I had the rope around me. I was carried to the top of the next swell and waved for Barry to pull me in. He did. I went back out to get the second ice chest and one of the preservers. Then we both leaned on the starboard gunwale of the boat to get her on her side. After that we were able to use the mast to lever the boat into an upright position. Barry secured the chests and duffel to the boat and we climbed in. I took a seat in the bow, chest deep in water. Barry sat in the stern. We were just light enough to maintain this arrangement as the submerged craft rose up and down with the swells.

"What now?" I asked, looking at the lights of Eleuthera ten miles away.

"I'm going to scull as hard as I can for as long as I can toward the island."

I looked at him skeptically as he started the back and forth motion with the tiller oar. But I didn't have any better ideas, and I began to vomit up the bitter salt water I had swallowed.

It was pitch dark now, the distant lights of Eleuthera our only comfort. Barry's efforts to scull us toward them didn't seem to have any effect. When it started to rain we lost sight of them.

The rain was cold and torrential. It completely obscured Barry, who was sitting only ten feet away from me. The rain persisted a long time and I felt entirely alone and helpless for its duration. When it let up I could see Barry again, as well as the moon rising on the eastern horizon, but the lights of Eleuthera were gone.

"It's that way," said Barry, pointing into the blackness and looking back at his illuminated compass. "Are you cold?"

"Yes," I answered.

He pulled his wet suit from the duffel and offered it to me, but
it was too small so he put it on and gave me his raincoat. He
located his flare gun and flares next. They had been in one of the
built-in compartments of the boat. He handed me the gun to put
in my pocket. Then he tried to give me the flares. They dropped
into the water. I reached to scoop them up before they sank out
of sight, knowing a single flare could spell the difference between life and death. One, two, three. I snatched them all and
placed them in my pocket.

Barry kept sculling as the moon rose higher. I held on in the
bow, heaving up spit and shivering in the seventy-five degree
water that lapped over my shoulders with every swell. Phospho-
rescent algae sparkled in the agitated water around us, and I
thought of the beautiful slides I'd made of their relatives from
Skagway, and how at home they were in this hostile, turbulent
sea. I thought how all life had come from Mother Ocean, and
how this might not be the worst way to die — in the bosom of
the sea that had given birth to all life on our planet.

"How are you doing?" Barry queried.

"Okay."

"I found some honey. Do you want some?"

"No thanks," I said. "You go ahead."

He gulped down a mouthful, and with renewed vigor sculled
us in the direction of the island. But it was futile. The sea was
taking us further out. We hadn't seen the lights for hours. Unless
another boat chanced upon us we were goners. I felt the flare
gun and flares in my pocket. They were still there.

Another squall enveloped us sometime after midnight. It
rained so hard that the sea was flattened for a time. Barry tried
to yell something at me during the deluge but I couldn't make
it out.

When the rain ended the moon came out in all her splendor.
She was waxing full this night, and directly overhead now. I could
have read by her light, and looking below in the water I thought
I could see the vague forms of sharks. The grim determination
on Barry's face was illuminated, too. He was sculling heroically,

waves washing over him, honey smeared around his mouth. I admired his tenacity but knew it was in vain.

I began to throw up again, heaving dryly, uncontrollably, weakening with every convulsion. I was hypothermic and slightly delirious. Wretched, I turned my attention to the moon, contemplating her serenity. How many times had I watched her rise and set, walked the countryside by her light, gloried in her romance, dreamed in her shadows? Was tonight to be my last dance with her? If so who would guess how I had died? Would it be Greg, whose father had met a similar fate? Would it be Jeff or Mike, Chester, or Steve? Would it be my mother, or my strange sister Nancy, who claimed to have mystical insights, and who, when I was a child, had whispered over and over in my ear as I slept that I would accomplish great things someday. Who would know my last thoughts? Who would know that when the end came there was no fear, only acceptance and understanding, only a joining with the eternal elements? I felt tired, I wanted to sleep.

"It's going to start getting light soon," Barry interrupted. "Let's try a flare. They show up better in the dark."

I took out the gun and loaded it.

"Go ahead," he said. With a glimmer of hope I pulled the trigger. The flare shot up a measly seventy-five feet, made a pop and glowed weakly for a few seconds. We were both disappointed.

"Shoot another one," Barry said. I did, with the same result.

Hoping that the first two flares had just been duds, I fired our third and last flare. If anything it shone more weakly than its predecessors.

As the wind increased, promising another squall, it was obvious to both of us that we were doomed. Barry ceased his sculling, rubbed his forehead in despair. I shivered. It was death by exposure for us unless a miracle occurred.

"Look!" cried Barry.

I twisted around, and there, just becoming visible behind a squall line was Eleuthera, no more than half a mile away.

"The rain must have been covering it all this time," reasoned Barry. He began to scull again. The wind conspired with him, and we were almost ashore when I saw the oddest sight. It was a cloud, or a shadow, or some kind of cloud shadow phenomenon, and it was in the shape of a perfect triangle whose apex reached up to the moon.

"What's that?" I said to Barry.

He turned to take a quick look, but was riveted by what he saw. I looked back, and this time fancied seeing three apertures in the cloud shadow that looked like eyes and a grimacing mouth. It was an ominous visage, but before either one of us could say a thing a big wave caught us off guard and flipped us over. It was a wild scramble all over again. We had quite a struggle righting ourselves, but we did, and by sunrise we had washed up on a sandy beach.

We dragged the boat above the breakers and collapsed into our wet sleeping bags in the shelter of some rocks. A farmer found us a few hours later and led us to his humble abode. There we were given a hot meal over which Barry gave me a peculiar look and asked, "Did you see the face in the cloud?"

CHAPTER THIRTEEN

CAL

*At current rates 5 to 10 percent of tropical
forest species will become extinct every decade.*
— Tropical Forests

It was good to feel solid earth beneath my feet again. To hear the sweet songs of land birds. To have food stay down in my stomach. To feel the warm sun drying out my wrinkled skin. I felt like the butterfly I had once rescued from a spider's web: I had a new lease on life, a second chance. I felt that I had perhaps been spared for some purpose. To write the *Fidel Fidel* script for my friend Joe?

The customs agent on the island didn't like Barry and me. He thought we were drug dealers, and closely inspected our wreck. When he found nothing he accused me of drowning my wife.

"I'm not even married," I protested. A radio call to Staniel Key confirmed my innocence.

Then the American ambassador, who had been informed of our calamity, called and asked us if we needed assistance.

"No," I said. Nothing of mine had survived but my B.C. and the shorts I had been wearing, but Barry had enough money to get us to Nassau, where I had left extra clothing and some cash.

Back in Nassau I considered flying straight home with my tail between my legs and the ocean out of my system. But I saw a handsome, sixty-foot research vessel docked at the Nassau Harbor Club and went to pay it a visit. It happened that the R/V Dragon Lady was a charter dive boat privately owned by a couple, Dan and Sue.

I introduced myself as Cal, having grown tired of my given name, and ended up telling them about my shipwreck. They invited me to dinner, during which they told me about their charter operation. Before dessert I had been hired as a deckhand.

A pleasant little girl named Terry made up the rest of the crew. She assisted Sue with cooking and cleaning in the galley. My primary duty was running the compressor that filled the Dragon Lady's twenty-four scuba tanks. I also swabbed decks, manned the anchor line, operated the skiff and occasionally took a turn at the helm.

Usually, groups chartered the Dragon Lady for diving in the Exumas, a chain of small islands forty miles southwest of Nassau. The group would fly into Nassau in the afternoon, come aboard for supper and orientation, and spend their first night seeing the sights of the Bahamian Capital. The next morning we would depart for the Exumas, passing Rose Island along the way. Rose Island was used to film the shot that opened the *Gilligan's Island* show.

We would reach Long Key by noon, anchor on her lee side and make a shallow dive. Then we'd do a drift-dive through a narrow channel dividing two keys. This was always a lot of fun. A current of six or seven knots ran in this channel, or cut. The divers would jump into the ocean at the channel opening and let the tidal rush take them to the windward side of the island chain. One diver always had a line and buoy attached to him. The Dragon Lady would follow the buoy through the cut and pick up the divers as they surfaced. After supper we would prepare for a night dive in the channel, waiting for the tides to change and the current to subside. These dives had to be perfectly timed, as a diver mustn't risk staying in the water over an hour and getting caught in a tidal flow.

In the morning we would sail to the drop-off, several hundred yards to the ocean — or windward side — of the islands, where the shallow Exuma banks ended. We would anchor on a ledge sixty-to-eighty feet deep and roll with the swells while the divers did their wall dive. Then we would weigh anchor and head southwest along the ocean side of the island chain, deep sea fishing for dolphin fish, tuna and mackerel. If we caught something we had to reel it in rapidly, lest it be set upon by sharks or barracudas. Sometimes we weren't quick enough and all we landed was the front half of our catch.

When we reached Cat Key we transited the channel and anchored on a reef in a protected inlet. This would be the site for a shallow dive, after which I would ferry people to the key in the skiff for some beachcombing.

In this fashion we would work our way down a fifteen-mile stretch of the island chain, turning back just short of Staniel Key, and stopping to dive on different reefs as we retraced our steps. Then it was back to Nassau to drop off our group and pick up another.

It was an enjoyable routine, and Dan and Sue were great to work for. Dan was easy-going and Sue loved the ocean. She and I often joined the groups on their dives. I would stick close to her and watch as she pointed out damsel fish defending their territory, surgeon fish with their razor-sharp caudal fins, porcupine fish that puffed up into pin cushions, and the golden, spotted moray eel that we could feed. I saw iridescent miniature reef-squid that changed color with their moods, and quarter-inch long transparent anemone shrimp living within the tentacles of their host, the long and skinny trumpet fish that blended in with sea whip coral by swimming on its head. I thrilled at big spotted eagle rays rising from the depths, at the colorful queen angelfish and the queer-looking parrotfish, whose bony mouths crush the coral they feed upon. A marveled at the sting rays buried in the sand below us, with only their eyes and gills showing, and the ugly hog fish that preyed upon the shellfish that it cracked open with the vise it had halfway down its throat. I saw tubeworms whose tentacles would retract when brushed against, nudibranchs, flame-lipped clams, different types of starfish, sea biscuits, and sea cucumbers that digested the organic matter in the sand they ingested. Schools of amberjack, French grunt, filefish, and friendly cowfish abounded, along with the deadly poisonous and well-camouflaged stonefish and the four-eyed butterfly fish that had a black strip running through its true eyes and deceptive eye spots on its tail fin.

After a dive Sue, her eyes and nose still encircled with the red ring the mask would make around them, would break out her fish guidebooks, and excitedly show us what she had seen, explaining the behavior and the ecology of the animals. She was a far cry from Bad Bob, and I learned about the wonders of the coral reef under her tutelage.

The night dives she took me on were especially educational. They were spooky at first; I imagined sharks swimming around us just outside the beam of our powerful dive light. But once I started to observe the nocturnal activity on the reef, I forgot all about my unfounded fears. It was at night, when the most of the fish were in a sleep-like stupor, that invertebrates like the brittle star came out. This was a disk with five protruding flexible arms, and it slithered across the coral and porous sponges from one recess to another in its search for detritus. More spectacular were the rare spotted rock lobster, the shovelnose lobster and the spiny lobster. They tiptoed across the sandy bottom on their eight legs like tiny armored cars. Translucent jellyfish pulsated above them, along with a fantastic collection of zooplankton, worms and larvae that were attracted to our lights like insects. When we shone our lights on the coral we could witness the drama of the zooplankton being captured by the carnivorous polyps that made up the colonial coral animal. These had tentacles like their anemone and jellyfish cousins, with which they would sting and engulf their nearly microscopic prey. The polyps were strictly nocturnal. During the day they remained sequestered in the relative safety of their calcium chambers while symbiotic algae passively carried on photosynthesis in their tissues.

The most beautiful of the night's performers was the coral-banded shrimp. It was a delicate-looking one-inch crustacean with alternating red and white bands, and was betrayed by its long and silky antennae that would often stick out of the crevice it was hiding in. The arrow crab was harder to find. Its body and needlelike nose rested on an undercarriage of legs like a rocket poised for takeoff. Other species of more conventional-looking crabs scurried over the coral and sponge reef complex, stopping here and there to pinch off bits of algae with their front claws and nibble them into bits with their mandibles. They were nervous feeders, always on the lookout for enemies. The larger ones were susceptible to attack from prowling octopuses. Sue knew the habits of all these creatures and enthusiastically shared her knowledge with me.

Dan taught me the subtleties of spear fishing. It was illegal to use tanks and spear guns in the Bahamas. The spear fisherman had to free-dive with a Hawaiian sling to achieve his goal. The Hawaiian sling consists of a slotted wooden handle and an elastic band. The shaft of the spear is passed through the handle slot and its end fitted into the sling. A diver must maintain his equilibrium with fin work while holding the handle with one hand and pulling back the sling and spear with the other. With good aim you could hit a fish from six feet away. But getting within that distance of the wary grouper or hogfish was not easy. These fish lived forty or fifty feet down. Holding your breath to get to that depth required some getting accustomed to, and stalking the fish was even more difficult. Dan was good at this, though. He would spot his prey and dive behind a coral head, then circle the coral and surprise the fish with a spear shot through the head.

Once he tried this with a large grouper at about sixty feet. His shot was a little off and his spear lodged in the body of the grouper, wounding it. The grouper swam into a hole, and Dan surfaced. He sent me down to finish the job. When I reached the grouper's sanctuary I took a shot. I missed, reloaded, aimed again, and this time found my mark. But by then I was running out of breath, and I made only a weak and unsuccessful attempt to pull the grouper from its hole before needing to surface for air.

Dan went back down, struggling without success to free our victim from its hole. He surfaced, and it was my turn again. But by now some bull sharks were becoming interested in our dilemma. Normally sharks never bothered us. It was only when we were spear-fishing that we were cognizant of the danger they posed.

I took a deep breath and descended. In my efforts to dislodge the grouper I pulled Dan's spear from its body. The fish itself stayed stubbornly wedged in its hole. When I surfaced my lungs were bursting. Dan took a gulp of oxygen, jackknifed at the hips and went down once more. This time he managed somehow to pry the grouper loose. As he ascended with it one of the larger bull sharks closed in. Dan reached me before the shark reached him, and I fended off our hungry guest with the end of Dan's spear. Dan threw our hard-won dinner into the skiff, and we both got out of the water before we had any real trouble.

Real trouble came off Andros. We had sailed there to accommodate a group of insane cave divers from Florida. They wanted to dive the underwater labyrinths of Andros Bight, where one of their number had drowned a year before, somewhere beyond the corkscrew. The corkscrew was a narrow passage four hundred feet into a cave where you had to take off your tank and push it ahead of you to get through. It was at depth of some hundred and sixty feet. This was rapture of the deep depth. The pressure at a hundred and sixty feet forces nitrogen into the bloodstream, causing nitrogen narcosis and disorientation. Cave diving was dangerous enough without adding nitrogen narcosis into the mix. Furthermore, Andros Bight was subject to tides. The divers had to time their trips into the cave with tidal changes, and if they got caught inside when a flood tide started they would find it quite impossible to make an exit.

Dan, Sue, Terry, and I would watch these intrepid spirits prepare for their dives with morbid interest, wondering how many of them would come back. They all had octopus regulators so they could share the air in their tanks with a partner in need. They had headlamps, underwater flashlights and reels of lines that they attached at the mouth of the cave. They wore small fins so they wouldn't stir up the sediment on the cave floor, and watches and decompression computers on their wrists so they could calculate their nitrogen status and avoid the bends on their ascent. To our amazement they all came back from their visit to their comrade's grave, and from their dives in the other Andros Bight caves where we anchored them.

The caves were something new to us, and Dan and I liked to don our scuba tanks and poke around their orifices for lobster. Toward the end of one dive we foolishly entered a wide-mouthed cave that descended straight down for fifty feet before angling off into the black unknown. Not intending to go beyond where we could see the cave entrance, we explored the dim recesses with Dan's flashlight, looking for lobster. We were almost out of air and about to head up when Dan's light failed. Total darkness surrounded us. We had gone too far inside the cave, and a panic worse than anything I've ever experienced took control of me. I shook my head back and forth looking for a hint of light and pressed my hands wildly against the cave wall trying to orient myself. Which way was out? Dan caught me by the elbow. He tugged me and we started to move blindly along the wall. I was breathing fast, using up the last of my precious air, and thinking the odds were fifty-fifty that we were going the right way. It got harder to draw air out of my tank, and soon I had sucked it dry. My time was up. What to do? Go on, trusting in Dan's sense of direction and possibly go deeper into the cave with him, or turn around and make a mad dash. I stuck with Dan, and seconds later saw the light of day. Dan was out of air too and cautioned me with hand language to make sure I exhaled to avoid an embolism as we made our rapid ascent. At thirty feet I rid my lungs of the last of my pressurized air, and fought the tremendous urge to inhale for what seemed like an eternity, until I broke the water's surface.

This experience soured both Dan and me on the sport of cave diving. We stayed aboard Dragon Lady the rest of the trip, and were not sorry to bid our charter group goodbye when we got back to Nassau. We had a two-week break before the next group flew in, and we immediately set out for Fort Lauderdale to re-supply. Sue flew ahead of so she could take care of some business while we made the passage. We had to anchor on the Bimini banks our first night. By dusk the second day we had made Bimini. We docked for the evening. Terry and I took shore leave.

We were hanging out in one of the bars Ernest Hemingway used to frequent, when an islander took issue with me over my attire. At six-foot four inches, I was much taller and bigger than the gentleman who was trying to pick a fight with me, and could probably have dispatched him with ease. But I had always found a way to avoid brawls, and was trying to negotiate a settlement when a cry went up from outside. We ran into the street and saw an orange glow on the horizon. A fire had broken out at the far end of the village. We rushed to the disaster with everyone else to see if we could help. When we reached the scene it was almost comical. The neighborhood was being burnt to the ground while an inept fire brigade was trying to stretch a hose from the nearest hydrant, a thousand feet away. People were screaming and gesticulating, giving advice to others and doing nothing themselves. Inhabitants of the thatched straw homes were evacuating their pathetic belongings as the wind spread the flames from roof to roof. I looked around me. This part of the village rested upon a spit of sand. With my hands, I began to shovel sand onto the nearest burning roof. It smothered the fire, and I instructed ev-

eryone around me to do as I was doing. Soon we had contained
the fire. The brigade came in with a water truck to mop up and
Terry and I returned to the Hemingway bar where I was treated
to drinks by the fellow who'd wanted to bash my brains in an
hour ago.

From Bimini it was a day's sail to Fort Lauderdale. We reached
our moorage in one of the canals, and were met by Sue and her
friend Bob Angove. A plumber, Bob had a wife, seven children
and a stunning mistress. He had made a fortune as plumber to the
elite of Fort Lauderdale, and then branched out into making an
underwater soft-core porn movie and training a world champion free diver. Over dinner he entertained us with anecdotes
about his movie. I told him I was in the movie-making business
too, and working on a script about the Cuban Revolution that
would set Hollywood on its ear.

"Bravo," said Bob, and we toasted each other.

We were busy for the next week, stocking up on food, paint-
ing the deck, overhauling the engines and scraping the bottom of
the hull clean. This last task was mine and was very interesting.
The ocean is full of larvae searching for a substrate to attach to,
and Dragon Lady had her share of hitchhikers. We were festooned
with algae, gooseneck barnacles, tube worms, anemones and
mussels. The pelagic larvae of crabs and shrimp had made their
home amidst this bounty and scrambled out of the way as I destroyed the fabric of their world with a paint scraper. When I was
finished the hull was clean as a whistle, and ready to be colonized
all over again.

Our return voyage across the Gulf Stream was rougher. I was
queasy most of the way, and I marveled at the thought of Barry
having sailed across it in nothing but a glorified dinghy. When we
got back to the Nassau Harbor Yacht Club I met Stuart Cove. He
had a diving operation on New Providence that specialized in
shark encounters, and had caught and handled the sharks used in
the James Bond movie, *Thunderball*. He had captured the big tiger
and bull sharks for the movie in the harbor entrance where they
followed the cruise boats into their docks.

While Stuart was visiting us I got word that a message awaited
me at the reception desk. It was from Joe, saying that he was
waiting for me to return with a script so we could get on with

our project. I called him and said I would fly back to Wisconsin after one more charter to the Exumas. That charter started two days later. When it concluded I regretfully said goodbye to my shipmates, who were turning right around to take out another group. I wasn't scheduled to fly out until the next morning so I bummed a room from John, a friend of Dan and Sue.

John was a veterinarian who had a nice home next to the harbor club. He had recently been divorced and had plenty of room for company. He had gone diving with Dan and Sue a few times and they had introduced us. While he was attending to his afternoon appointments I strolled through the streets of Nassau one last time. I saw two very attractive, light-skinned women in front of me.

I caught up with them and said, "Be careful of the sun down here, it can give you a bad burn before you know it." They regarded me. I was tanned bronze from my months at sea, my hair was long and blond, and my body was well toned. They seemed to approve of me and thanked me for my advice.

As we walked into their hotel for a drink they told me their names, Karina and Matar. I told them mine, Cal. They were from Copenhagen, and had just arrived that day. They were planning a two-week stay, and had all kinds of questions about the island. I did my best to satisfy their curiosity, and offered to take them out for dinner that evening. They looked at each other for a moment.

Before they could say no I said, "Wait a minute, I have a friend. His name is John. He's a vet here on the island. We could make it a foursome." They nodded their assent and I phoned John from the lobby. He was reluctant at first, but when I described how beautiful the women were, he agreed to the enterprise.

We picked up the girls at seven, and they were a sight to behold. Karina, tall and blond, wore a blouse and a tight-fitting skirt, and had highlighted her model's face with just the right amount of makeup. But compared to Matar she was only so-so. Matar looked absolutely ravishing. Her breasts were recklessly exposed in a revealing, ankle-length dress that was cinched with a belt around her lovely waist. A slit running up almost to her hip showed off her gorgeous legs to devastating effect. The sandal-style heels she wore were three inches high, and put her perfectly shaped feet and pretty toes on display. I offered my arm to escort her to the car, leaving Karina to John.

Dinner was a complete success. John drove us in his Jaguar to a romantic and intimate restaurant where we drank wine and dined on lobster. He was a charming Englishman and seemed accustomed to being in such company. I managed to be urbane also. As we were polishing off the second bottle of wine I suggested we go for a moonlight swim in the harbor. The girls readily acquiesced. After dinner we drove them back to the hotel for their swimsuits, and then to John's house. We had one more bottle of wine there, and the girls broke out two marijuana cigarettes, which we shared. Then we all changed into our swimwear.

John took us out in his boat to the middle of the harbor where we had our privacy. He cut the motor. The moon shone overhead and the girls looked lovely in its magical light. They felt the water with their hands, then stood up and removed their bikinis. John raised his eyebrows, but I followed the girls' example by taking off my trunks, and jumped into the water with them. They urged John to join us.

"I better stay in the boat," he responded.

So it was just Karina, Matar and me in the water, naked, uninhibited, playful and amorous. I don't know if it was the wine, the weed or the moonlight, but it all seemed right and natural. We caught each other up in embraces, and when it became obvious to Karina that I was more interested in Matar, she left us to ourselves and climbed into the boat with John. My last evening in the Bahamas turned out to be my most enjoyable.

CHAPTER 14

LOST SOUL

*Indigenous populations in the Amazon Basin have declined
from 9 million in 1500 to 250 thousand in 1990.*
— Trees of Life: Saving Tropical
Forests and their Biological Wealth

Joe was anxious to see me when I got back to Wisconsin. He hadn't gotten very far with his story-board, but he wanted a look at my partially completed script of *Fidel Fidel*. We went over it together. He said yes to some scenes, no to others. I nodded in agreement with his decisions. The Santiago sequence, Castro's first major attack on an army installation, was good. So was the thrilling conclusion in which his freedom fighters stormed Batista's Palace of Mirrors. The secret police torture scene was satisfactory as well. But Fidel's pre-revolution speech wasn't stirring enough. At the time, he had been an idealistic law student protesting against a corrupt government, and I needed to portray that better.

All in all Joe was pleased. I couldn't say the same. I had anticipated a trip to Mexico City when I had left Dragon Lady and Matar. Instead I discovered that Joe was still estranged from his family and was repeatedly visiting the theater to watch some movie called *Star Wars* that had come out that summer. He said he was learning a lot about film techniques from analyzing the blockbuster.

While I was away he had taken a job at the wax museum in a tourist town called Wisconsin Dells. He got me hired by the bar next door to the museum, and we lived in a shabby cabin he'd rented. It was fall and the tourist season was over so we weren't very busy and had plenty of time to work on our movie. How-

89

ever, Joe rarely did anything with his storyboard, and I had hit a wall on the script. Our collaboration degenerated into a sorry bout of drinking and bluster. We would go out to the taverns every night and talk about the great things we were going to do. Sometimes Joe would talk about his '60s rock n' roll band that almost made it big. He would tell me about the fine venues he played, the drugs he took, the parties he threw and the endless stream of pretty young girls he bedded. I listened raptly, envious of his sexual prowess, a prowess he still had and used with the women that came into our bars. He was like a magnet to them. Our nights usually ended with him taking home the girl of his choice.

Eventually this grew old for me. I pressed Joe to get on with the storyboard, to make his peace with his family so we could get down to business. But Joe procrastinated. As long as he had some sort of roof over his head, a drink in his hand and a woman in his sights, he was content. I began to wonder if he had family connections in Mexico City. Maybe he had never been that serious about the scheme, maybe it had been all talk. I began to regret leaving the Dragon Lady and Matar, realizing I had been an idiot to abandon the woman of my dreams and forsake my crewmates to pursue a Hollywood phantom.

Our partnership broke up the night Joe stole my date. I had just met a girl the previous afternoon in the bar where I was working, and with considerable difficulty had convinced her to go out with me. Our evening was concluding at a late-night restaurant where we were having breakfast when Joe walked in. At first I was glad to see him. I introduced him to my companion and he sat down, grinning sexily. He turned on the charm immediately and I began see its effect on the girl. I tried to get him to tone it down but he ignored me.

"I must be mistaken," I thought. Joe had plenty of women of his own. He didn't need this one, too. But he did. When breakfast was finished she left with him. The next day I quit my bartending job and returned to Madison.

Mike was there to greet me, and wasn't surprised at what had happened. He had only met Joe once but he hadn't liked him a bit.

"A false messiah," Mike said of Joe. Now he asked me what I

was going to do. I told him I was driving to Fort Lauderdale. Maybe I would hook up with Dragon Lady again. He wished me luck, and I wished him the same. He was about to go into the navy and try to get his wings as a jet fighter pilot.

My dented old Chevy took me to Fort Lauderdale without incident. When I got there I learned that Dan and Sue were in the Exumas. I sent them a message through Dan's sister, who ran the landside part of the business and was in radio contact with Dragon Lady. Dan asked me how I was doing and told me he had found another deckhand. So it was back to Madison for me. After a few disillusioning months of bartending there I set out again, this time for San Diego. I had some notions about crewing on a yacht bound for the Fiji islands, but San Diego was a bust.

By the time I returned to Wisconsin it was spring. In my travels I had noted some beautiful residential landscaping and thought landscape architecture might be a rewarding career. I interviewed and was hired at McKay's Nursery, the biggest ornamental tree and shrub operation in the state. It had a staff of architects who designed planting arrangements for the customers who bought McKay stock. I wasn't added to this staff right away. I had to work my way up. My first task was to clean the old farmhouses that the migrant workers would soon be moving into. It was a disgusting job. The houses had been left in a filthy state the previous fall. Refrigerators had spoiled food in them, congealed grease covered the stoves and hordes of mice would scatter when I lifted the piles of garbage that had been left over the winter. I was glad to finish this assignment and move on to fieldwork

The fieldwork was grueling. We spent the days digging up row after row of trees and shrubs for spring sale. McKay's guaranteed these plants, and many species had to have their roots dug up in big balls of earth that were then bagged in burlap sacks. The foremen who oversaw our fieldwork taught me a lot about the various plants we uprooted. Still I was glad when I was promoted to truck driver, and began to deliver the plants to our customers.

It was good to be behind the wheel of a big truck again, driving down the road enjoying the scenery from the high perch of my seat, following a route through the springtime countryside that had been mapped out for me by Clarence, McKay's gay dispatcher, stopping to unload my plants and chatting knowledgeably with clients about the proper planting and care of their stock. I thought I had found my vocation, and pictured myself creating fantastic, biologically sound landscape designs that would be as unique as the structural architecture of Frank Lloyd Wright. I was disabused of this notion when the delivery season ended in late June and I was given a tour of the architects' musty studio, where several designers were grinding out yard plans. All the plans were variations on the same theme, using the standard trees and shrubs that McKay's liked to grow and sell. There was no soaring of the imagination here, no radical innovation, no creative genius, just a drab, factory-like atmosphere that promised nothing more than a paycheck at the end of the week. I quit the job and bid adieu to Clarence, the only friend I had made during my apprenticeship at McKay's.

Meanwhile Mike had graduated from Officer's Candidate School and had commenced his pilot's training. He suggested a military career to me. The camaraderie, uniforms and travel of a soldier's life appealed to me. I saw an Air Force recruiter, took his test, scored high on it, and was accepted into the OCS program beginning in November.

The program was conducted at Lackland Air Force Base, outside San Antonio, Texas. I was bussed there and deposited in a barracks with fellow officer candidates. It was exciting at first. Everyone wanted to be there, and all were motivated by the prospect of getting their gold bars.

Right from the start an *esprit de corps* was promulgated. Each platoon was given a nickname and competition was encouraged. Recognition was given to the platoon that marched best, or completed the obstacle course first, or scored highest on written exams. But it was also understood that the platoons were a part of the same team, that we were all training to be Air Force officers, that there was a bond of honor among us.

This was all fine and dandy for a while. However, the getting up every morning at 4:30AM, the fastidious cleaning of our rooms late every night, and the boring classroom lessons on military etiquette grew tiresome. It was worth enduring for those of us who were looking forward to graduation and advanced training in their fields. But I had been peg-holed to become something called a "disaster preparedness officer." To my dismay this seemed like it would consist mostly of shuffling papers. Two weeks into the program I self-selected out of the Air Force. Our platoon had lost its best athlete and marcher.

On the bus ride home to Wisconsin I figured I'd go back to school, take a few education courses and get a job teaching biology. I registered on the Madison campus for the spring semester and moved into Mike's apartment with him. He had washed out of flight school after coming tantalizingly close to earning his wings, and felt as lost as I. He had a car and a bedroom, though. I was reduced to sleeping on his couch and relying on city buses for transportation.

Mike found a job working for the Capitol Police, a rinky-dink security outfit that paid minimum wage. I talked him into enrolling in the local tech school's police science program. With each other's moral support we began to look forward to the coming year. Our spirits had even risen enough to throw a New Year's bash in the apartment's party room. It was spoiled by a winter storm, however, that discouraged all but one of our guests from attending. Mike was bummed about this and wanted nothing to do with the festivities being planned for the party room by some girls who lived on the other side of our apartment complex (we had met them as we were clearing away the debris of our sad little affair). I had to literally drag him to their party. But he was glad I did. There he met his wife. Her name was Mary, too.

School started and I got a part-time job at Paco's, a Mexican bar and restaurant. My education courses were just interesting enough to keep me engaged and Paco's paid my bills. If I could hold on for two semesters I'd have a teaching license and could search for a real job. Mike was planning to graduate and apply for meaningful work within a year also. At the end of a long day of classes and security work in the nearby Capitol Building he would come into my place, wearily order a plate of tacos and a beer, and talk about how things would get better once we finished school. Then I would close up the bar and we would drive back to the apartment.

This dreary sort of life went on into the spring, until one night Lynette and her mother visited Paco's. The usual crowd of arrogant, good-tipping and mostly fat attorneys were bellying up to the small bar, but there was still space for these two ladies. They sat down and Lynette's mother ordered a wine cooler for herself and a coke for Lynette, who was only eighteen. Somehow Lynette and I started talking. She was in her last year of high school and couldn't wait to graduate because everyone there was so immature. She wanted to be a social worker. She didn't care about making a lot of money; she just wanted to do something interesting and worthwhile with her life. I chimed in, saying that I wanted to teach and continue to write. I told her that I wasn't materialistic either. That I didn't care a whit for the big fees, expensive cars and grand houses that the alcoholic lawyers I poured drinks for always raved about. I eloquently regurgitated the rhetoric of noble philosophers, espoused the idealistic sentiments of poets, and shared with her my aspirations for doing something that would make this a better world. "It's not what a man *has* that matters," I told her, "it's what he *has done.*"

We started going out and she was a wonderful young woman. But I was listless and full of self-doubt. It was a time in life when I just wasn't ready to become seriously involved with anyone. What did I have to offer anyhow? I was penniless, sleeping on Mike's couch, and had to borrow his car to take Lynette on a date. Lynette didn't concern herself over these things. She was in love with me. It didn't matter to her that I was destitute, had no definite plans for the future, was nearly seven years older than she and was still spinning my wheels, lost and confused. Though she was only eighteen, her perception was keen. She saw a special quality in me. She saw potential. She saw something in me, I guess, that I still didn't see in myself. But finally, frustrated with my soul-searching and lack of commitment, she ended our relationship, kissing me softly on the lips and saying, "I hope you find what you're looking for."

CHAPTER FIFTEEN

MY GIFT TO GREG

*At present 140 million people comprising
1,000 indigenous groups live in rainforests.*
— The Nature Conservancy fact sheet

I took some summer education courses, and in the process found out about opportunities for teaching abroad. This appealed to me, and though I didn't yet have a license I sent letters of inquiry to several far off places. To my surprise Sam Velazquez phoned from Puerto Rico and offered me a job in a small private school in San Juan. I accepted it and flew down to the U. S. commonwealth in late August.

Sam picked me up at the airport and showed me the apartment he had found for me. It was a *casita* — a small house behind a large home — intended as a maid's quarters. It suited me fine and I moved in. Then Sam gave me a tour of the school. It was a picturesque assortment of small buildings bordering the beach and shaded by palm trees. This was where I was to teach middle school science and math, and oceanography.

The next day we had an in-service meeting. I met the rest of the staff. They were all women, most married to men who made substantial amounts of money. Rose Alvarado's husband was an airline pilot, Marcie's a successful comedian, Sally's an economist, and Enid's an engineer. These women weren't teaching to support themselves as I was, they were doing it to keep busy, or because they loved children, or because their own children were enrolled in the school and as teachers they could get free tuition for them.

After the meeting we were allowed to go to our rooms to

prepare for the classes that would start the following day. I wasted some time rehearsing my opening speech at a podium and practicing how I would write Mr. Calhoun on the blackboard. Then I set up the two twenty-gallon saltwater aquariums that were to be the centerpiece of my oceanography course. After that I entered the names of students in my grade book. Beautiful names like Soraya, Gissele, Migros, Gabriel, Branwen and Desmond, names that would become faces, and faces that would become individuals with unique personalities and unique talents and unique needs. I was looking forward to my first day of teaching.

That day did not go very well. My classes were ridiculously small but I was so inept at dealing with the onslaught of the students' questions and their unpredictable behavior that it seemed the circus had come to town. The pompous and esoteric speech I had prepared for the enlightenment of my charges went unappreciated, the students giggled as I mispronounced names, and made disparaging comments in Spanish, a language I had failed to learn in college. At the end of the day I confided in Sally, the middle school English teacher, that my classes had been a fiasco. Sally told me I would have to stay one step ahead of these adolescents if I wanted to survive.

"Be organized," she urged. "And prepared. Always have some learning activity ready to go. And don't let them talk out of turn, in English or in Spanish. You have to establish discipline in your room. Once you do that the learning and thinking can start."

I followed her advice, and by the end of the week I had established an ascendancy over my twelve-year old pupils. I did, after all, tower over them, and could, when needed, feign great anger by slamming down a book or banging on my desk with a fist. This always reestablished order.

After an early September hurricane that nearly wiped out our school I began taking my oceanography students snorkeling on the shallow, degraded reefs just offshore. We observed many kinds of marine life and collected specimens: club urchins, swimming scallops, anemones, box crabs, mantis shrimps, sergeant major fish, bristle worms and a juvenile moray eel. The habits of our captives were easy to study in the aquarium. I think the students were most fascinated with the urchins, which would migrate across the glass surfaces using dozens of suction-cupped tube feet.

My oceanography class was second in popularity only to Noleen's gym class. Noleen, like Sally, Mary Wander and I, was an import from the states. She was younger than I, single, and lived across from me in the second story of a house. She was arrested by the police one day as she officiated a volleyball game in the schoolyard. This news spread like wildfire through our student body, and rumors ran rampant about what her crime had been. Sam had to go to the jail to rescue his physical education instructor. It turned out that the broken-down wreck of a car she had bought had once been reported stolen by its previous owners, and the records had never been cleared up. Noleen was released but remained infamous as the car bandit for the rest of the year.

Sometimes Noleen would give me a ride to school in her unreliable junk heap. But she was a late riser and I usually preferred to walk the half-mile to San Juan School by the Sea. The residential streets I walked were tree-lined and often fresh from the evening rain, and an invigorating wind blew in from the ocean. As I ambulated to work I would regard distant El Junque, the mountain that loomed over the eastern half of Puerto Rico and always seemed cloud-covered. It beckoned to me, but I had no means of getting to it.

After school I would return to my casita by the same route. There was a lime tree outside my front door. I would pick one of its fruits and squeeze the juice into a late afternoon rum and coke. Restored, I would change into swim trunks and stroll to the beach four blocks away. I dunked in the ocean and then went for a long barefoot run. At the end of the run I would do a hundred sit-ups and two sets of fifty pushups. I had picked up the habit of exercising in the Air Force and couldn't shake it.

Marie, one of the few unmarried teachers at our school, saw me running down the beach one day and nicknamed me "Superman." I preferred to think of myself as Tarzan, but Superman wasn't bad, and I began a flirtation with Marie. She lived in a stylish home owned by her absent fiancée. She had a brand new truck and big powerboat at her disposal. We planned to take the boat out one weekend but we had some trouble with it so we caught a DC-3 to the Virgin Islands to do some snorkeling.

The DC-3 is a classic two-engine propeller aircraft that's reminiscent of a more romantic age. It was the plane that left Bogart bereft in the fog in Casablanca, the plane that Indiana Jones crashed into the Himalayas, and the plane that was the backbone of the air cargo industry in the 1930s, '40s and '50s. It has beautiful lines and a rugged design that has kept it in service in out-of-the-way locales like Alaska and Puerto Rico. Our DC-3 flew low over the ocean and landed us safely on St. John's. Marie and I had a good time snorkeling there, and returned home with a case of Bacardi that had cost me a paltry twenty-two dollars.

A few weekends later Marie drove me up to El Junque in her fiancée's truck. This was the first time I'd ever been in a tropical rain forest and I was confounded by the overgrowth of vegetation. The mist-enshrouded tree ferns conjured up visions of an epoch long past, when slimy amphibians ruled the earth. Growing on the forest floor beneath them was a befuddling array of lush plants, and on the branches of trees I couldn't name, epiphytes flourished. There were herbaceous vines that wound around everything, and woody lianas, the kind that jungle explorers cut with their machetes to get a drink of water.

The richness of sounds was as perplexing as the botany. Strange bird-songs filled the air. The croaking, chirping, clinking, beeping, peeping, buzzing, trilling, pleating and ringing of unseen insects and frogs was nonplusing, and gurgling streams and crashing waterfalls added to a jumble of noise that almost made me lightheaded. The pattering of rain mingled in as we completed our hike through the park. When we passed a field station on our way down the mountain I told Marie I wanted to hold our spring camp there.

By spring our staff was a tightly knit family. Sam was our softhearted patriarch, Sally our understanding counselor, Noleen our irascible coach, Enid our artist, Marcie our muse, Mary our social conscience, Marie our problem solver and I, as Noleen liked to call me, our "big man." The aforementioned staff persons, along with Sally's husband, Bill, were the camp chaperones, and under my authority, for Sam had entrusted camp to me.

Our students numbered forty-five souls. They were sixth, seventh and eighth graders. They were very excited to be away from home and required a lot of settling down in their cabins the first night. The next morning we did our plot studies in the forest, a not very memorable project I had cooked up. But the students enjoyed being out-of-doors, and things picked up in the afternoon when Noleen held her Camp Olympics. The events included relay races, balloon tosses and tugs of war. That night after dinner and chores we had a campfire around which we told the children scary stories. Then we allowed them some free time to play their favorite game, "kick-the-can." I never fully understood how this game was played, but it involved teams, and hiding and seeking, and flashlights and, of course, kicking a can. A few of the tamer students didn't participate in the game; rather they investigated with me the bizarre insects that were attracted to the camp lights. The three-inch beetle we saw was worthy of mention in their journals — the written record they kept of their camp experience.

These journals were somewhat amusing. Mostly the students talked about the cabins they slept in, the games they played at night, how they got all got muddy on the hike up the mountain with me, and how they had to police the grounds, mop floors, wash dishes and clean bathrooms. Excerpts from the journals were compiled in the newsletter that came out after we returned to San Juan. A review of camp food by Rene was typical: "Well, food in camp was good but not as good as at home. The food wasn't good but anyway I ate it all because at the time they gave it I was very HUNGRY."

The second morning we did our study on the stream that ran by camp. Everyone fell in the water at one point or another, and to the students this was the highlight of a supposedly academic proceeding. After lunch we went on a long hike and got caught in the rain. This was followed by a well-deserved supper and the camp talent show held in the old pavilion. Marci, Marie and Enid orchestrated the night's festivities, which commenced with Sam playing *Tenderly* on his saxophone. Next the seventh graders sang a song that parodied our staff. Then Mary and I sang Gordon Lightfoot's *Wreck of the Edmond Fitzgerald* to the accompaniment of her guitar. The night's entertainment ended with a dance number by Soraya, Gissele and Gretel-Salazar, done to Barry Manilow's *Copa Cabana*. It won the competition hands-down.

Greg had come to visit me in January, long before camp was held. It was great to see my old friend. A lot of water had passed under the bridge since we had last dived together in the Bahamas, and I was lonely in my casita. Once the school day ended I saw little of the staff. Marie had thought better of her indiscretion with me. Sam was busy administering the school and raising a family. Noleen spent a lot of time with her church friends. Marcie traveled with her semi-famous husband in circles beyond my means. Enid and Mary were newlyweds. That left only Bill and Sally, who invited me over to dinner with them and their two darling daughters a few times and had taken vacations with me to Mona and Culebra Islands, but still had their own lives to lead. So Greg was a welcome guest, and I gave him my bedroom and slept on the couch.

When I was at school Greg contented himself with reading books, walking the beach, doing our laundry, shopping for groceries and mulling over his next move at Panzer Blitz, a stupid war game at which I consistently annihilated him. At night we would play this game or Cribbage and usually have a few drinks. Greg didn't care for my rum colas. He favored Sloe Comfortable Screws, which contained a blend of orange juice, vodka, sloe gin and Old Fashioned Comfort.

Noleen dropped in one night. I introduced her to Greg, and he introduced her to his concoction. She developed a taste for it and for Greg's company. It wasn't long before she was visiting regularly, drinking Sloe Comfortable Screws, playing three-handed Bridge with us, adding her soprano voice to our renditions of *You Are My Sunshine* and *Paint Your Wagon* — "Where am I going? I don't know. When will I get there? I ain't certain." — and joking with Greg about how she loved sloe comfortable screws. But the two of them could never quite take the next step. Noleen had some religious scruples and Greg lacked experience in these matters. The affection Noleen had for Greg did have its advantages, though. She loaned us her car and we set off to explore the island.

We drove up into the central mountains first. Then we headed down to the southern coast, and camped on "Dead Battery Beach," as Greg liked to call it because the car wouldn't start there. The next day I named the place "Porpoise Beach" for the porpoise I saw offshore while Greg fiddled with the car. After that we visited El Junque, then drove to Farjado and caught the ferry to Culebra. This was a dry and desert-like island that had been used as a firing range by the United States military during World War II. We rented a jeep and followed a rough gravel road to a seldom-visited beach. There, to our delight, we discovered the hulk of an old Sherman tank. The main point of our trip to Culebra was to do a night dive, though. Greg had never done this and I wanted to show him what a reef was like in the dark.

That evening, as the light of day was fading, we piloted our skiff to a safe anchorage and waited for the night shift to take over down below. As we sat and talked about old times the lights of St. Thomas began to shine east of us, and a red moon rose above the horizon. "We'll have some moonlight for our dive," I commented.

A little nervously Greg swished the water, which made the diatoms around his hand sparkle. "Nice and warm," he said.

"You'll love it," I reassured him. But I was a little apprehensive, too. Diving off a big boat like Dragon Lady with a large group of people on a familiar reef was one thing. This was another. The inky blackness of the sea held the unknown for us. Anything could happen in its murky depths. Greg and I were, after all, land-dwelling creatures of the day. To us the sea was an alien world, and our primordial prejudice against the ebony of night made it seem more alien yet.

"Men who would brave any danger in the day," I thought, "can be shameless cowards after sunset."

Greg took a deep breath. "I'm ready," he announced. We opened the valves on our tanks, checked our regulators, tested our waterproof flashlights, put on our masks and flipped over backwards into the ocean. We descended to a depth of thirty feet and followed the reef line, occasionally turning our lights off to better see the light show the abundant bioluminescent algae gave. We stopped by a huge head of brain coral and took pictures of each other with Greg's underwater camera. Then we continued on, Greg poking and prodding the reef with his oversized screwdriver, jabbing at the poor fish hidden in their crevices and goading along the hapless lobsters he encountered. He had always been the scourge of the reef with that goofy old screwdriver, and his mechanic's heart loved it dearly.

A half-hour into our dive we turned around to swim back to the boat. The moon was high enough now to give us some illumination, so toward the end of our dive we turned off our lights. As our eyes gradually adjusted to the dimness, the ghostly reef became distinguishable. This was the way the reef looked to its inhabitants as they furtively sought out food and mates. This is the way it had looked for eons. The way it had looked when primitive trilobites had had their fling. The way it looked before the cephalopods had become extinct. The way it looked when mammals had returned to the sea to evolve into seals and dolphins and whales. This was the sea in all her glory and mystery. Pensively, we took a last look around and surfaced.

"Where's the boat?" Greg inquired after making a three hundred and sixty-degree turn.

I squinted myopically, unable to see the details of any object clearly without my glasses. "I don't know." All I could see was the brightly moonlit and distant shoreline of Culebra.

"You don't suppose it slipped its anchor and drifted off do you?" he speculated.

"I hope not. Look over in that direction."

"Nothing," he said after a moment. "I think we anchored over there."

He scanned the opposite horizon.

"Here we go again," I thought, "just like the time when we were in the woods picking cranberries in Alaska and disagreeing over which way the dormitory building was."

"No," I said. "I'm sure we anchored over here."

"Nope," he insisted stubbornly, and continued to look off in the wrong direction. "We should have left a lantern on the boat."

With this bit of wisdom I agreed. I had led us far astray during the dive, carelessly losing track of our position, and instead of taking us back to the boat I took us further away from it. Then again maybe I hadn't, maybe the boat's anchor had worked itself free and the boat had drifted away. I couldn't be certain. But I did have a rough sense of where the boat should be, and it wasn't where Greg was looking. "I'm inflating my vest," I said.

We both did, and discussed our situation. We could probably swim to shore in two or three hours, sooner if we dropped our tanks, providing we didn't run into any currents or hungry sharks.

"Look this way again," I requested. Having thoroughly surveyed the rest of the ocean Greg accommodated me. He looked and looked and looked. Finally he said he thought he saw it. Yes, he could just barely make out a white speck. It was the lightly colored outboard motor on our skiff.

"It's about a hundred and fifty yards away," he said.

We swam to the boat, somewhat shaken but none the worse for wear. The next night we dove again, but took the precaution of leaving a lantern light on the skiff's bow. The following morning we caught the ferry back to Farjado, and from there drove home to San Juan in Noleen's pitiful jalopy.

Greg had a week or so of vacation left, and a few nights after we had returned to San Juan the Lathams invited Noleen and us over for dinner. Sally cooked a delicious meal. Then we broke out the board game I had invented. It was called "The Primate Evolution Game," and I wanted to test it out under field conditions. The object of the game was to evolve from tree shrew to tarsier to ape to Homo erectus to Homo sapiens. Each player began with five populations of tree shrews. They would move their populations around the board acquiring traits by drawing cards such as stereoscopic vision and opposable thumb, and throwing dice to add to their brain size. At the end of each round the players negotiated to breed their populations with those of other players. In this way they could get the traits they hadn't been lucky enough to draw from the cards. When populations mated their brain size was averaged. This meant that you could gain brain size by mating — or lose it. If your populations didn't acquire the necessary traits and brain size to evolve to the next level they fell behind and had a greater risk of drawing an extinction card. The winner of the game was the one who had the most breeding populations reach the Homo sapiens level.

From the start Greg had good fortune in acquiring traits, but his dice throwing left something to be desired. He soon found it difficult to find partners to breed with because nobody wanted to dummy down their brains by mating with him. As the game went on this became a standing joke, and much merriment was made at his expense. Noleen was especially coquettish, refusing his earnest proposals to mate with her, but telling him that as soon as his brains increased to a reasonable size she would consider reproducing with him.

This never happened. Greg's brain size lagged behind every-

one else's and he was left stranded in the early part of the Ceno-
zoic era to evolve in isolation, if he could, or go extinct if he
couldn't. We others didn't care; evolution is a cruel business and
we selfishly concerned ourselves with procuring bipedal loco-
motion, tool-making ability, fire, language, more brains, cave art,
and a sense of humor. Bill eventually won the game by reaching
the lofty status of human being with four populations. Greg
achieved something of a moral victory by doggedly building up
the brains of one of his populations and shepherding it through
the ice ages until it finally became sapient. The rest of us had long
concluded our part in the game and moved on to various conversations by the time he accomplished his goal and let out a
shout of "Hurrah!"

On Greg's last night in Puerto Rico, Noleen and I threw a
party in her apartment. It was turning maudlin when I proposed
that we go for a swim in the ocean. Greg thought this a fine idea
but Noleen balked. She was more of a sunbather than a swim-
mer.

"Just come along then," I inveigled.

She said, "Okay."

It was late when we got to the beach and there was nobody
else around. The sound of the waves rolling onto the shore and
the tradewinds blowing through palms were the only things to
be heard. Salt spray filled the air and the gritty sand felt good
between my toes as I spread out a blanket for Noleen to sit on
and said to Greg, "A la nude?"

"But of course," he gallantly rejoined, having lost his inhibi-
tions due to the drinking of one too many Sloe Comfortable
Screws.

I think Noleen was alarmed by this unanticipated develop-
ment. She bashfully looked away as we removed our trunks. But
I had gauged her mood and inclination correctly. As Greg and I
headed into the surf I glanced back to see her watching us. When
we returned she averted her gaze again until Greg and I had
picked up our towels and started to dry off. Then she fixed her
eyes on Greg, admiring his sturdy legs, his partially exposed hips
and buttocks and his robust and hairy chest. Greg, oblivious, was
laughing unaffectedly and shaking his head to get the water out
of his ears, acting completely natural, which made him all the

more attractive. If I had been a woman at that moment I would have desired him, and there was no doubt in my mind that Noleen was besotted. I had only to evaporate into the Cimmerian night to make it happen now, and I did. I slipped away without their noticing, and in the predawn hours of a warm, seductive Puerto Rico evening Greg gave away his virginity.

Jatun Sạcha, along the Rio Napo in the Amazon of Ecuador.

CHAPTER SIXTEEN

DEPRESSION

*Indigenous peoples in Northwest Amazonia
use over 1,300 plant species as medicine.*
— The Healing Forest

When the school year ended I left San Juan, expecting never to return. There was no future for me there. Sam's school was a wonderful place but I had earned a mere 6900 dollars for my entire year of teaching — less than the campus handyman was paid. On that amount I would never be able to make a life for myself, never be able to move out of a casita, buy a car, find a wife and raise a family. San Juan School by the Sea was for privileged children and happily wed women who thought of teaching as a sideline, not as a career. Furthermore, I had begun to feel confined by the smallness of the island, and isolated by a language I didn't speak and a culture I didn't fit into.

Back in Wisconsin I moved into Mike's new house in Deforest, a suburb of Madison. He had built it while I was away, through a government program called Self-Help Housing. I missed out on the construction of the house but was of great assistance to him in planting his yard with numerous trees and shrubs.

Mike had gotten a job with the Verona Police Department and was planning to get married the following spring. He had really shot ahead of me: house, job, fiancée. I went back to summer school, manipulating my program so I would be certified to teach in Wisconsin by August. My new advisor didn't like it. He thought I should do a semester of student teaching. But before I had gone to Puerto Rico I had made my previous advisor give me a letter stating that my year of teaching in San Juan could be substituted for that.

"Highly irregular," my professor complained. "We've never waived this requirement before."

But I wouldn't allow him to derail me, and he reluctantly gave me my credits. In the end it didn't matter; I applied to several schools around Madison and wasn't even called for an interview. As September approached I gave Sam a call. "Have you filled my position yet?" I asked. "What kind of raise can you give me?"

We settled on a salary of 7,200 dollars, and I caught a flight back down. As soon as I got off the airplane I knew I'd made a mistake. I found myself an apartment and started ticking off the two hundred and seventy-five days remaining before I could go home. This is like being in prison, I began to think, and envied Bill and Sally, who had returned to their home in Delaware, and Greg, who was in Alaska, and Mike, who would soon be a married man. Two hundred and seventy-four, two hundred and seventy-three. I did some work in my classroom. It seemed small and squalid now. The aquariums looked dingy, the desks dilapidated, the lab equipment inadequate and the textbooks worn and outdated. "San Juan School is a backwater," I reflected, "a slough far from the cutting edge of education."

Day 272 — Friday. In-service day. Sam was talking about the challenges of a new school year and the blessings of being a teacher, a mentor of youth, a sharer of knowledge, a planter of seeds. He talked of the necessity of nurturing students as if they were saplings growing up toward sunlight, of treating our pupils as if any one of them could grow up to be the next Albert Einstein, Ludwig Von Beethoven, William Shakespeare or Winston Churchill. I gazed out the window at the oppressive ocean, inattentive, despondent, thinking that if only another hurricane would hit the island maybe the school would be destroyed and I would be released from my responsibilities. Deeper and deeper I sank into my melancholy.

Day 271 — Saturday. I went for a morning walk that failed to revive my spirits. Dejected I returned to my dreary apartment wondering how on earth I was going to make it through the weekend, not to mention the next nine months. A heaviness overtook me. I slept the afternoon away and felt terrible when I awoke.

Foggily I considered returning to Wisconsin. No, I couldn't do that. School was starting on Monday. I had signed a contract. People were depending on me. But the idea had taken hold of me. I became obsessed with it.

"I should call Sam first," I thought in a haze. "No, he would try to talk me out of it. He would force me somehow to stay and fulfill my obligations."

I called the airlines and made reservations on the next available flight, Sunday evening. After that I began to feel guilty. I was expected to show up Monday morning to meet the bright, shining faces of Gissele and Soraya, who would be eighth graders just beginning to blossom into beautiful young ladies, of Rene, the smartest but most spoiled boy in our school, of Gabriel-Garzia, who loved oceanography so much that he wanted to take the course again, of Migros, of Gretel-Salazar, of Anthony and all the rest. How could I not show up? Maybe it was better to see it through after all. My head spun as I debated the pros and cons of deserting San Juan School by the Sea.

I slept fitfully that night and rose the next morning unrefreshed and morbid. I decided to pack my things. I was going to get out of there no matter what. It was beyond endurance to stay. I caught my breath at the thought of really going. Was freedom so close at hand? Was it all just a bad dream that would end in a few short hours when I boarded my flight home? Could it be that easy? Yes, it could, and I was energized by the prospect of making a clean escape, of shedding my onerous duty. What did I owe the school anyhow? What did I owe Sam? A year of my life? No. My life was mine to do with as I pleased, and it pleased me to leave. I took one last walk, touring the neighborhood, congratulating myself on a resolve to be liberated from the shackles of San Juan School.

At dusk I called a cab to take me to the airport. It picked me up under cover of darkness and sped me secretly to my destination. But when it pulled in front of the terminal I had a change of heart.

"No, this isn't right," I thought, "this isn't worthy of me. It's a craven thing to do."

I told the taxi driver to take me back to my apartment, and for a short time felt satisfied with my noble act of self sacrifice. But the closer we got to my apartment the more I regretted not having followed through with my plan. I began to feel claustrophobic, began to feel like I was suffocating. I told the driver to turn around and take me to the airport. He shrugged his shoulders and did so. I was okay now. I would be airborne in two hours. I would call Sam when I got back to Wisconsin and tell him, "Sorry." Then I would seek out, with more determination this time, a teaching position in a place where I belonged. But halfway back to the airport I began to waver again. Was San Juan such a terrible place? Hadn't I made it through the first year? Hadn't there been good times? Were two hundred and seventy days such a price to pay for keeping hold of my integrity, my self-respect? Couldn't I hack one more year in Puerto Rico, and then return to Wisconsin with my head held high?

"Turn around," I instructed the driver.

As we headed back I felt that I'd made a fateful decision; that somehow, someday this night would have repercussions, that whatever I might suffer in the coming months would be for a reason, a higher purpose, perhaps, than my own happiness. Despite this sentiment, I couldn't help the feeling of despair that rose up in my throat, the feeling that I could not spend another night alone in that dreadful apartment. I could not face another dawn on this inhospitable island, or the sick, weak feeling that I lacked the strength and the character to do the right thing. Mentally exhausted and emotionally spent, I told the driver one last time to reverse his course. I unloaded at the terminal, caught my flight and returned to Wisconsin.

I experienced a total collapse when I got home, overcome with remorse and guilt. I couldn't believe I had done what I had done, forsaken my post, abdicated my honor, broken my word. What had the children thought on Monday morning when Mr. Calhoun failed to materialize? How had Sam coped with the catastrophe? What irreparable damage had been done to the school's reputation?

Distraught, I dwelt upon the perfidious act I had committed and the worry I was causing. No one would be guessing that I had perpetrated a heinous crime, and betrayed a trust. They would be searching for me, calling the police, wondering what mischance had befallen me. I had to at least let them know I was all right. I called and got Sam on the phone. He sounded relieved to hear me. Then, sobbing like a baby, I confessed my treachery to him, expecting him to condemn my behavior. Instead Sam comforted me, assuring me that everything was under control at the school, that I shouldn't be so upset, that what mattered was my well-being. The soothing voice and kind words of this gentle man helped me get a grip on myself, and I realized I should have discussed my feelings with him before things had gotten so out of hand. But what was done was done, and I had to try to pick up the pieces of my life.

I bought a cheap, old station wagon and began to substitute teach in several schools around Madison. I soon found out how special San Juan School by the Sea had been. The schools I was subbing in were public institutions geared toward mass education. The atmosphere in them was impersonal compared to that of San Juan School. The hallways were crowded with strange faces, the teachers' lounge replete with educators who had burned out, people who had been teaching too long and had become cynical with their profession and boring to their students, the classes large and unruly, the views out the windows mundane, the curriculum stifling.

At the end of the day I would tell Mike how rotten it had been, how it was a miserable way to make a lousy thirty-five or forty dollars. He would sympathize and offer the hope that things would get better. But they didn't. I began to hate the sound of the telephone ringing at 6:30 in the morning, the voice of the principal summoning me to work, the visit to the school office where I was given the room number of the teacher I was subbing for, the lesson plan I was to implement and the class list of pupils I felt no connection with.

I grew nostalgic for San Juan School by the Sea and unhappier with myself. I had fled a little paradise, abdicated my place there and stained it with sin. For a while I fantasized about how I would redeem myself. On the living room wall of Mike's house I would project the photographs I'd taken in Puerto Rico and swear that I would go back there someday after I had accumulated a fortune, and donate it all to the school. Then I would drink a rum cola to dull the pain I was feeling, then another and another. More than once Mike would come home from the swing shift at

Verona to find me passed out on the floor, the fan of the slide projector whirring, a picture of palm trees on the wall.

November closed in; its relentless gray clouds hung low over the Midwest. I stopped subbing, investigated some overseas job openings, sent a few letters out and sank into apathy. Mike worried about me. He told me I should get some help, and that there was something wrong with me. He was right. What a mess I had made of my life. I thought of all my mistakes, all the bridges I had burned; White Pass Railroad, McKay's Nursery, Dragon Lady, Matar, the Air Force, Lynette, and now San Juan School by the Sea. I was a worthless soul, all right, a quitter, a failure, an idiot who kept fouling up. The world would be better off without me, and I couldn't think of any reason not to kill myself. I drove my beat-up station wagon into Mike's garage, shut the door, and left the motor running.

"What a sordid way to die," I thought, rum bottle in hand, half inebriated. It would have been better to have drowned in the Devil's Triangle or in that lake in northern Wisconsin, or to have had my head squashed under the tire of my mother's car, or to have never been born at all.

How did Sophocles put it? "Not to be born is, past all prizing, best: But, when a man has seen the light, this is next best by far, that with all speed he should go hither, whence he hath come."

I sat in the dark, breathing in the noxious fumes, calm, resigned, grateful. I was so weary of life, so tired of self-reproach, so void of spirit, so empty. In a few minutes it wouldn't matter any more what I had or hadn't done at life's crossroads. It wouldn't matter that I had disappointed and been disappointed. The hemoglobin in my blood would become saturated with carbon monoxide and lose its ability to deliver oxygen to the cells that comprised my being. I would pass out, my brain cells would start to die, and it would be over. Mike would find my body as rigor mortis was setting in, shake his head in pity and call the undertaker. I would be buried in the ground, forgotten, and the earth would continue rotating through the eternal heavens.

Was there anything I had left undone? I pondered. Should I write a note, leave an explanation, bid adieu to my friends and family? What would Greg think when he heard of my demise?

What would Jeff and Mary, who now had five children, make of my suicide? My mother, how would she take it?

I quoted the last stanza of a Robert Frost poem: "The woods are lovely, dark and deep, but I have promises to keep and miles to go before I sleep, and miles to go before I sleep." Did I have any promises to keep? Did I have any unfinished business to attend to? Was I about to make the same error I had made that night in San Juan, to opt for what I thought was the easy way out?

I considered my choices. I could let events run their course, and like my Aunt Violet and Uncle Pearlie die by my own contrivance. Or I could pick myself up by the bootstraps and begin anew. I remembered I had the phone number of The International School of Nicaragua, one of the schools I had written to. What did I have to lose my calling them? Their notice had said they had an immediate opening. I went into the house, not bothering to turn the car off. I was going to take a long shot and call the school. If they hired me, fine. If not I would go back to the garage and face the final curtain. I dialed the number. A secretary answered and put me through to the headmaster. Yes, he had received my resume, and yes he still needed a science teacher. Could I come down right away?

I hung up the phone after agreeing to be his man, went to the garage to turn off the car, sobered up and made arrangements to travel to Nicaragua, which had just come under communist rule and was in a chaotic state. My tenure there lasted one week. Quitting is like committing murder; it becomes easier and more natural each time you do it. I retreated to Wisconsin once again, and after a period of incapacitation sought out the council of a psychiatrist.

"Any history of manic depression in your family?" he asked me, after I had related my problems to him.

"Yes. My dad had episodes of depression that were treated with electroshock."

"We don't do that anymore. We use medication. Any other family history?"

"My mother had a nervous breakdown. My maternal aunt shot herself and I had a paternal uncle who hanged himself."

"Anything else?"

"I think my sister Nancy is schizophrenic. But that could be because she fell out a second-story window a couple times and cracked her head."

"Hmph," he remarked, thinking no doubt that he had entered into fertile country with his new patient. "Manic depression is hereditary. That's what you have. Your symptoms are classic. The disease just hasn't manifested itself until now. We'll put you on some medication and see what happens."

I took lithium to control my mood swings, and a sedative to help me sleep at night, and began feel good enough to function. I went back to subbing, made the best of it, and moved out of Mike's house so Mary could move in. I was now reduced to living with my mother. But that worked out because when spring came I was rehired at McKay's to drive trucks, and mother lived closer to Waterloo. I had no illusions about working for McKay's permanently, and while there I submitted my teaching résumé to several schools that had positions becoming available in the fall. A Monte Hottman contacted me, and I took a day off of work to do an interview with him.

Monte, a short, balding, hard-working and teacher-loving superintendent liked me. He perceived that he had found quite a catch, an unpolished talent that would enrich the science department of his high school. He apologized for being able to offer me only a part time position, but hoped I would consider joining his staff anyway. No other schools had responded to my queries so I accepted employment with his Dodgeville School District, and said farewell until August, when I would begin a new phase of my life.

CHAPTER 17

THAT'S NOT A KNIFE

Over 2,000 plants have been identified
by scientists as having anti-cancer properties.
— Trees of Life: Saving Tropical Forests
and their Biological Wealth

It was not quite true that no other schools had responded to my queries. There had been one, a small missionary school in Kenya. It was located on the shore of Lake Victoria in a remote district that would have been very interesting to explore. According to the headmaster, just getting to the school could be an adventure. At any other time in my life I would have jumped at an opportunity like that, but after the debacle in Nicaragua I didn't trust myself. I played it safe and missed what I thought would probably be my only chance to see Africa.

Instead, after the delivery season with McKay's ended, and before my stint with Dodgeville School District began, I took a trip to Montana. Jeff was stationed in Great Falls and I had talked him into going backpacking with me in Glacier National Park. When I drove up to his house, Mary, Jeff and their five children were sitting on the front porch waiting. The four youngest, all boys, had been born within a span of six years, and this was the first time I had ever seen them. But it wasn't long until they were climbing all over me and calling me Uncle Bruce. I liked this. After what I had recently been through it was good to be in a house full of rambunctious children.

It was good to see Jeff again, too. He and I had grown up together. As children we had built fleets of model ships and blown them up with firecrackers, constructed forts out of bottle caps and garrisoned them with toy soldiers and attacked with rubber band ballistics, had snow ball fights in the winter, and water-balloon battles in the summer.

In puberty we had abandoned such childish pursuits to catch crayfish by sinking our skinny arms up to their pits in the mud burrows that the crayfish thought were impregnable, and to write and produce a spoof on a cassette — which we titled "Dr. Gonad" — complete with sound effects and theme music. Jeff had been the voice of Dr. Gonad and several other characters. I had been the voice of the oversexed spy whose mission was to foil Dr. Gonad's evil plan to release a virus that would sterilize mankind.

Our youth had not been all fun and games, though. Jeff's stepfather, a sergeant at Truax Field, had agricultural ambitions. He established a truck garden and a roadside vegetable stand on his property. Jeff and I were his laborers. Jeff's older, pampered half sister was his vegetable stand manager. Jeff toiled in the fields because he had to, and because he had been promised some of the profits from the stand, which in the first year at least, he never saw because all the money went to buy Liz a horse. I worked alongside him because he was my friend, because he couldn't play until the tomatoes were hoed and because his mother would reward me with chocolate donuts that she brought home from her bakery.

Jeff's stepfather had gone insane, the garden overgrown by the time we reached high school, and after settling our quarrel over the crayfish incident Jeff and I became closer friends than ever. His legacy to me when he went into the service was an obsolete, twenty-pound, four-track tape player that he screwed to the under dash of Rambler.

Two days after my arrival in Great Falls Jeff and I departed for Glacier. We arrived at the welcome center late in the morning. While Jeff wandered around the place gawking at the stuffed animals I cross-examined a park ranger about the grizzly bears. He told me there were a lot of them, that they could be dangerous and that a woman had been chased up a tree a week ago on one of the trails. I asked him if there was a wilderness campground in the vicinity of the treeing.

"Well yes," he replied, "but nobody has been going up there lately."

I registered us for a site at this camp, Jeff grabbed a few information brochures and we drove off to the trailhead. When we got there the small parking lot was devoid of any other vehicles, and Jeff asked, "Is this the right place?"

Jeff was no outdoorsman. His idea of a park was a place where crowds of people held picnics on neatly manicured lawns bordered by a few stately trees and a lake brimming with fish that wanted to be caught.

"Yes," I said. "Let's pack up."

We put on our heavy backpacks and walked to the trailhead. A sign at the entrance gave the name of the trail, and in big red letters warned, 'Beware, This Is Grizzly Habitat.' Jeff was taken aback. He had not anticipated that our little expedition would take us through bear country.

"Is this really the right place?" he asked, anxiety in his voice.

"Sure is," I cheerfully replied. A few days spent in a deep wilderness where encounters with North America's largest and most ferocious carnivore were possible was just what I was in the mood for. I wasn't suicidal anymore, but I wasn't looking forward to spending the rest of my life in dull little Dodgeville either, and the thought of being eaten by a bear really didn't bother me that much.

We headed up the trail, my long legs taking big, easy strides. Jeff followed me and took little steps with his short legs that retarded our gait. Rugged granite peaks rose up around us, a distant lake shimmered in the afternoon sun and great pines and spruces lined our path. The air was fresh and sharp, the blue sky cloudless. After an hour plus of hiking we stopped at a viewpoint that offered us an especially scenic vista.

"What's that sound?" Jeff asked.

I strained my ear and heard a low growling.

"I think it's a bear," I whispered. The growling stopped, then started up again. It didn't seem to be getting any closer.

"What do we do? Should we run for it?"

"No, you can't outrun a grizzly," I answered him. "There's a knife in my back pack. Get it out."

I bent at the knees so Jeff could rummage through my pack.

"Come on, hurry up," I said keeping my voice low.

"I'm hurrying, I'm hurrying."

"It's in a big black sheath with a flap over the handle."

The growling stopped, then started once more. Jeff redoubled his efforts.

"Got it," he said triumphantly.

He handed me the sheathed knife, and stepped to my rear. In contrast to me Jeff had a lot to live for, and he wasn't shy about taking whatever precautions he deemed necessary to guard his safety.

I unsheathed my knife. It was an eight inch beauty, and completely useless for anything but sticking bears in the belly. As I stood on the trail, knife at the ready, I reflected that it would be a shame if I had to kill one of these magnificent animals. Outside Glacier there were practically no grizzlies left. Before the coming of civilization they had ruled the west, roaming mountain and prairie with impunity, revered by the native tribes for their strength and feared for their temper. The long rifle had changed all that, and now the bears were restricted to Yellowstone and Glacier, unwelcome and shot if they strayed onto ranch land outside the parks.

The growling stopped again. I puzzled. Was this bear about to attack or not? Was it waiting for us to make a move? Was it even aware of our presence? I cocked my ear. A gust of wind disturbed the trees. There was a growl. The wind gusted again. Another growl. "It's a tree creaking in the wind," I told Jeff anticlimactically.

It was a long hike to our secluded campsite. We didn't get there until nearly dusk. I set up the tent and gathered firewood while Jeff tried his luck fishing in the nearby lake. He didn't catch anything, and he petulantly began throwing stones at a convoy of ducks, who indignantly moved out of his range. I think this gave him a sense of security, a feeling that he could keep nature at a distance. I walked over and related to him the story of a former big-league pitcher who had beaned a charging grizzly and killed it with a rock not much bigger than the stones he was throwing. Jeff looked doubtfully at his projectiles and tossed them into the lake, and we repaired to our fire to roast our fat chicken on a spit.

After our greasy meal we sat by the fire, resting our tired bodies. Jeff took out a brochure and started reading it by flashlight. "Hey," he said, "we're not supposed to cook meat out here. They say the aroma attracts bears."

"Too late now," I reassured him.

"And we should wear bear bells so the grizzlies can hear us coming when we walk down the trail."

"I don't have any, do you?"

"Listen to this," he said disconcerted. "If a bear attacks the best thing to do is roll up and play dead."

"If a bear attacks us I'll take care of it with this."

I pointed the wicked blade of my knife at him.

Then he fretfully added, "A hiker was killed just last year by a sow protecting her cubs."

I put some more logs on the fire, tied our food up in a tree and retired for the evening. Jeff joined me in the tent long after I had surrendered myself to somnolence. He shook me on the shoulder, waking me up, and telling me I shouldn't sleep in the clothing I had worn while cooking a meal, he was in his briefs.

"Get some shuteye," I mumbled.

He disturbed my slumber several more times that evening, alerting me to sinister sounds emanating from outside the shelter of our flimsy tent, surely wishing that he was back in the missile bunker he'd manned, snug as a crayfish in its hole, with a nuclear warhead between him and any enemy threatening violence.

In the morning he discovered that a chipmunk trespassing in our camp had probably been responsible for the night noises that had so alarmed him. He chased the mischievous little rodent around the tent with a stick, finally throwing it at his nemesis, whereupon the interloper retreated with a squeak into a hollow log. Then, red-eyed from lack of sleep, he went to the lakeshore to stretch and throw more stones at the ducks. Meanwhile I performed my morning ablutions and fixed a hardy breakfast. We ate and set out for a walk along one of the streams that fed the lake, Jeff with his fishing pole, me with my knife tucked into my belt.

"There should be some nice trout in this stream," I observed to Jeff.

He concurred, and we continued on our route unencumbered by our packs, enjoying the scenery and the weather of another

fine day in the high mountains. Jeff forgot about his night's dis-
comfort and began to babble about Air Force politics, base housing, smelly diapers, Mormon dogma and how much he had liked
Okinawa. In the middle of his discourse I froze in midstep and
motioned him to be silent with an urgent wave of my left hand.
Ahead of us, just twenty-five feet away, a large brown body was
emerging from the forest and onto the trail.

"It's either a moose or a grizzly," I said to myself. "If it's a
grizzly we've got trouble."

I reached my right hand down to my knife and unsnapped the
sheath cover. The grizzly stepped out and paused, broadside on
the trail. Amazingly it was unaware of our presence, and I took
advantage of its heedlessness by letting out a blood-curdling roar.
Simultaneously, I ripped my knife out of its sheath and raised it
menacingly over my head. Caught by surprise and startled by my
belligerence, the bear turned on its haunches and sped away with
the utmost haste. For ten seconds I remained in my stance, adrena-
line pulsing through my arteries. Then I felt a weakness at the
back of my knees, and found it hard to stand. I turned around. Jeff
was withdrawing from the scene, fishing pole still in hand, and if
I hadn't yelled for him to stop I believe he would have continued
his flight all the way back to Great Falls.

We examined the bear tracks, noting the creature's impressive
claw marks, then resumed our hike, me extolling the virtues of
my Buck knife, Jeff rationalizing his act of self-preservation by
saying he had been going to get help. We came to a waterfall with
a pool beneath it that looked trout-worthy, and I left Jeff angling
while I scouted the surroundings. When I came back Jeff was
comfortably seated on a big sunny rock, his line in the water, his
mind at ease, the night's consternation and day's peril all behind
him. I approached him from behind, the sound of my footsteps
muted by the waterfall.

"Should I?" asked a little voice inside me, and I closed the
distance between us.

He looked so innocent at that moment, so boyish, so at peace
with the world that I was almost dissuaded. But the temptation
was too great. I seized him around the chest with my big paws
and imitated the bellow of an enraged bear. Jeff's body convulsed

and the spasm launched his pole high into the air. He whipped his head around in absolute terror, his heart beating like a jack-hammer under my pseudo-bear hand. It took him a second to focus on me realize that his death and dismemberment were not imminent.

"Funny," he said sarcastically.

When our time in Glacier ran out I dropped Jeff off in Great Falls and headed back home. I was driving up the entry ramp of an interstate just outside Tomah, Wisconsin when I spied a dis-gruntled hitchhiker sitting in the grassy island. It looked as if he had given up hope of ever getting a ride, and he was peevishly stabbing at a piece of cardboard with his jackknife. I stopped.

"You need a ride?" I yelled.

He peered at me with narrowed eyes and gruffly said, "You bet."

He folded his knife, grabbed his battered suitcase and ambled over to the car. He opened a back door and threw his suitcase rudely in, then opened the front door and bounced into the seat. I started up the ramp again and accelerated onto the freeway.

"Where are you headed?" he demanded.

"Madison." I didn't ask him where he was going. By the looks of him it was nowhere. He had tattoos on his arm, a scar on his neck and the demeanor of an ex-convict.

"I'm going to Adams. Where is that?"

"It's about twenty miles north of the Dells."

He sat in silence for a moment, ruminating. Then he told me he wanted me to take him to Adams.

"It's out of my way," I said.

He gave me an ugly look. Then said, "You're going through the Dells aren't you, it's not that far out of your way."

"I've been on the road all day, I'm not driving an extra forty miles to take you to Adams."

He leaned back in his seat, annoyed, dug into his pocket and took out his knife. He opened it and patted his hand with the flat of the blade in an intimidating manner. "It won't kill you to take me to Adams."

I saw where this was going. I would give him a ride to Adams, because it wouldn't kill me. Then when we got there, or at his insistence turned off on a lonely side road along the way, he would say it wouldn't kill me to lend him twenty bucks, and then, perhaps, it wouldn't kill me to lend him my car.

"Okay," I acquiesced. "Let me get my map out of the glove compartment. I want to make sure of the best way to get to Adams."

I reached across him, opened the compartment and, instead of removing a map, laid hold of my eight-inch Buck knife. I closed the glove compartment and emphatically placed the knife in my lap. "I think you're getting off at the next exit," I said.

He folded up his impotent little jackknife and didn't say another word.

I think Hollywood somehow heard about this confrontation and adapted it for a scene in *Crocodile Dundee,* where a street tough tries to hold up Dundee and his girl with a switchblade. The hood tells Dundee to hand over his money, Dundee shakes his head.

"What's the matter with you man?" the hood says. "This is a knife."

Dundee smiles at him, takes out his huge Crocodile knife and says, "That's not a knife...*this* is a knife!"

CHAPTER EIGHTEEN

DODGEVILLE

Chocolate, vanilla, black pepper, cinnamon, paprika, nutmeg, coffee, tea, ginger, lime, orange, grapefruit and many other spices, flavors and fruits come from the rainforest pantry.
— Rainforest: Tropical Treasures

When I arrived in Dodgeville for teacher orientation, Monte Hottman had good news for me. A full-time position had opened up in the middle school. The salary was almost twice that of the part-time high school position I'd been offered. It was mine if I wanted it, but I didn't want it. After inspecting the middle school science facilities I decided the high school was a better place to work. Besides, I liked the high school's biology teacher, Gari Walz, with whom I would be sharing a room, so I turned down the extra money and joined the senior staff.

To cut expenses I moved into a farmhouse with Jim, a math teacher and the football coach. I paid forty-five dollars a month for my upstairs bedroom, which had no heat and was very cold on winter mornings. But I liked it out in the country. I would take our landlord's dog for walks in the woods where we would encounter everything from coyotes to badgers.

As the school year progressed I settled into my duties as a part-time biology teacher. The room I taught in was well ordered and in good condition thanks to Gari's scrupulous supervision. He never allowed students to abuse the lab desks, or the lab equipment, or their books, or each other or him. His classroom was an orderly place where students learned whether they liked it or not, and his thorough curriculum ran the gamut from grasshopper dissection to reading Aldo Leopold's *Sand County Almanac* — the conservationist's bible — that spoke eloquently of nature and the need for a land ethic.

When I first met Gari he was naked from the waist up, digging postholes on a hot August afternoon for a wood fence to encircle his school arboretum. He caught his breath to tell me Dodgeville was a decent town, and that we had a good high school science department. Next he told me about nearby Governor Dodge Park, where he worked as a summer naturalist. He told me about its rocky bluffs, tree lined lakes, pioneer history, wildlife and Indian lore.

"You'll like living here," he concluded, then told me that Jim Detwiller was looking for a roommate, and invited me to his house for a beer.

In addition to teaching biology I assisted Barb Thompson, the Special Education teacher. Barb's room was a bright and sunny place, and Barb was a warm and sympathetic human being. She loved her developmentally disabled students and created a safe and pleasant environment for them. Much of their time was spent listening to the radio while they chatted lightheartedly and did repetitive piecework for a local business called Walnut Hollow. They were paid for the work and it taught them the skills they would need if ever they were to enter the adult workforce.

Officially my job was to teach these students science, a subject they found uninteresting. I emulated Barb instead and put them to work. I would take our B-5rs — as they were called because of the designation of Barb's classroom — to the school's new greenhouse, and teach them to sow seeds and transplant seedlings. I would also take them outside to plant seedlings in a tree nursery we had established, and to tend our beehives. By spring we were ready to start a little business. We put up a booth at the farmer's market in Madison and sold the honey we'd harvested and the flowering plants we'd raised. We also planted more seedlings in our nursery, little trees destined to be dug up again and planted on school grounds according to a landscape plan I designed.

In January Barb requested that I go with her to the auditions for *South Pacific*. She wanted to try out for a part but was too nervous to go alone. I assented and accompanied her to nearby Mineral Point, where The Shake Rag Players executed their performances in the High Street Theater, the oldest theater in the state of Wisconsin. When the director called her name she turned to me and said, "I can't do this."

"Sure you can," I said, but she wouldn't budge from her seat. "Will you try out if I try out?" I asked.

"If you go first," she responded.

I told the director I wanted to audition for a part. She nodded and I got up in front of everyone, dismissed the pianist, and belted out "Maria," from *Paint Your Wagon,* a cappella. I thought the song had always sounded good when Greg and I harmonized, but I stank up the place, and the director waved me offstage as a few people applauded me for my verve. Barb, encouraged by my example, tried out next, singing *Bali Hai.* She was given the role of Bloody Mary. To my surprise I was also given a part — that of Captain Bracket, the crusty old commander who did a lot of yelling and ordering people about but didn't sing a single note.

Quite by accident I was back in the limelight, in a community theater production of a musical this time. The cast was huge. I met a host of interesting people: Dick, a tall, dark and handsome farmer with a baritone voice that made the local women swoon; Tom, an aspiring artist who'd quit his high-paid furniture-making job to devote more time to the bizarre figures he carved; Jim, who raised Arabian horses on his ranch and sold them for fifty thousand dollars apiece; and Cindy, the wisecracking costume maker who lovingly ridiculed Dick for his exaggerated ego.

Most interesting of all, however, was Roland. He played Luther Billis, the comic lead, and was incredibly funny onstage. Offstage he was something of a stick-in-the-mud. He rarely joined the rest of us at the local tavern where we gathered after rehearsals, and when he did he would drink only Cokes. He was witty enough when he wanted to be, but overly serious, I thought, and too ready with his criticism of society's ills. He lived in downtown Mineral Point, in the upstairs studio of an old stone building he was restoring, didn't watch television, and read everything he could get his hands on. He was liked and respected, but had an aloofness that kept people at a distance.

A few weeks before opening, Cindy, who was also in charge of publicity, solicited our biographies for the program. I created an uproar by suggesting that the program include a commentary I had written. It read:

> *South Pacific* takes place on a tropical island para-dise in the midst of World War II. Sadly, forty years later, tropical settings throughout the world are dis-appearing. The vast equatorial rainforests are being exterminated by over-logging, cattle ranching and unsustainable farming practices. If exploitation of these fragile wildernesses continues, the jungles of the world will be but a memory before the next generation of children matures. This will not only mean the doom of half the world's exotic wildlife, but will also result in the extinction of many North American songbirds that winter in equatorial lati-tudes. Therefore, we urge you to join us in our deep concern over this and other environmental issues and to observe Earth Week, April 18–24.

Some of the cast and crew were supportive, others said it was inappropriate to place such an editorial in the program, and that it didn't represent everyone's views. After one of our re-hearsals I made a speech stating that people needed to know about what was happening in the tropical rainforests, and that plays came and went but once the rainforest was gone it would be gone forever. This split The Shake Rag Players asunder. The progressive camp thought my cause was just, the conservatives wanted to kick me out of the play and send me back to Dodgeville where I belonged. Roland remained outside the controversy until he came up with the thoughtful suggestion of placing my epistle in the program's paid advertisement section as an announcement sponsored by concerned members of our communities. This met with universal favor, and harmony was restored to the set.

The following summer I returned to the Bahamas and spent

my vacation working on Dan and Sue's new boat, Sea Dragon. Then it was back to Dodgeville in late August with a carousel full of slides for my classes. I hadn't arranged for a place to live so I took up residence in the school's lounge. Larry Dunning, the principal, discovered me shaving in the lounge bathroom and asked what was going on. I confessed that I had been squatting on school property. Larry, like Sam, was one of those administrators who truly cared about his teachers. He took me home with him and set me up in his half-basement, which had been used as barbershop in the past. It had a little bathroom, a bedchamber and a small space that he converted into a kitchen for me. The square footage was about equal to my casita in Puerto Rico, and seemed spacious to me after a summer on Sea Dragon, where I slept in a cramped bunk in the bow.

With a roof over my head I began another school year, employed on a three-fourths time basis. Gari and I continued to share a classroom but our teaching styles differed greatly. He would plow through the subject matter with exactitude. I would gloss over it at times and experiment with activities that sometimes worked and sometimes didn't. We complemented each other nicely; Gari kept me from getting too far off the beaten track of our curriculum, and I pestered him with ideas that made his instruction less tedious.

When we were released from school to attend the state teachers' convention, Gari and I went together. As had always been his practice he attended sessions and conscientiously logged his time on the first day, and I tagged along. But on the second day I began to get restless, and urged him to duck out early with me. Other teachers did this routinely, but not Gari. He was the consummate professional. To him a convention was an opportunity to learn more about the latest teaching methods, to have erudite conversations with colleagues from other schools, and to review the materials displayed at the booths. In his mind it was heresy to skip out, and he was well known for attending each convention to the bitter end.

But I was persuasive. I whispered in his ear that we had seen enough, that the convention was winding down, that we had faithfully listened to the keynote speaker, sat through a multitude of sessions, examined the booths and touched base with all his friends.

"But what about the drawing?" he countered. "You don't win if you're not here."

"Drawings are just a gimmick to make dopes hang around after all the good stuff is over," I explained.

"The prize is a computer. I need one."

"Gari," I said, exasperated, "fifteen thousand people registered for the drawing. What are the odds that they're going to pick your name out of the hat? I know this really good Chinese restaurant."

Hungry, Gari reluctantly followed me out of the convention hall, looking over his shoulder to see if he was missing anything. I got him into the car and we drove away. Over a delicious dinner at the Golden Wok I praised us for the initiative we had taken, and chattered on about how stupid it was to be manipulated by advertising and incentives and things like drawings. Gari seemed on the point of agreeing with me when two teachers from our elementary school entered the restaurant and, upon seeing us, rushed over excitedly.

"Where were you?" one of them asked.

"Huh?" he said, not understanding the terrible import of her question.

"The drawing. They picked your name."

Gari gave me a look like he was going to throw up, then asked the teacher what had happened next.

"Well, everybody searched around for you, including Mr. Dunning, but when they couldn't find you they drew another name."

To his credit Gari didn't blame me for his not getting the brand new computer that he desperately wanted but couldn't afford. Everyone else on our staff did, however; I became notorious as the bad influence that had led the punctilious Gari Walz astray, and both of us were ribbed about the affair for a long time.

During spring break that year I had a manic episode. The previous fall I had co-starred in a Shake Rag production of a mediocre comedy called *The Second Time Around*. I told everyone at the time that I could write a better play. When we were released for Easter I made the attempt. I took the composite novel I had outlined for my university project and adapted it for the stage. It took a week, and I hardly slept, ate or washed, so engrossed was I with writing *The Sinister Minister?* When I finished it I put it in a drawer to cool off, and resumed teaching until school let out in June, when I caught a plane for Australia.

Dr. David Neil and the author at Jatun Sacha, Ecuador

CHAPTER NINETEEN

BIONIC BRUCE

*Two-thirds of all the world's rain falls in the Amazon Basin.
You can canoe out 100 miles from the river's mouth and
still scoop up fresh water, and there are more species of
fish in the Amazon than in the Atlantic Ocean.*
— Save the Rainforest fact sheet

During my second summer crewing for Dan and Sue, I learned about The Australian Institute of Marine Science, AIMS. It was located in Townsville, Queensland, and conducted research on the Great Barrier Reef. Some of the top marine biologists in the world carried on their work there, and the institute was always looking for qualified divers to assist them. I wrote to the institute and was offered a volunteer position for the summer of 1983. I accepted.

A few days before I was to depart for Australia I found out that the Self-Help Housing program was coming to Dodgeville. I checked it out and learned that I was eligible to build my own house with them that summer. The program required no down payment and only forty hours of labor a week under a supervising carpenter. Furthermore, Farmer's Home Administration would underwrite the mortgage, and my payments would be tied to my income level, which was still pretty low. It was a great deal, but the lure of Australia was too strong and I forewent the opportunity to become a homeowner.

The first thing I did in Townsville was to arrange for a place to stay. A friendly Aussie told me that there were cheap and respectable lodgings to be had at Doreen's. I procured a room there and contacted the chief diving officer at AIMS to let him know where

I was. He picked me up the next day and we drove to the institute. It was situated on Cape Cleveland, thirty miles from Townsville. En route I got my first look at wild kangaroos. The officer, John Hardman, fitted me out with diving gear, gave me a schedule of the research I would be participating in, gave me a tour of the institute and introduced me to some of the scientists.

One was an American marine biologist, Dr. Janice Thompson, who specialized in the study of sponges, and was very enthusiastic about her chosen field. She told me that ancient reefs had been dominated by a genus of *Porifera* that was as hard as coral. She patiently explained that many sponges are symbiotic, require sunlight, and that large species filter hundreds of gallons of water a day as they feed on plankton. Then she explained that the sharp, microscopic silicon and calcium carbonate spicules of sponges come in all shapes and sizes, and that they function as both a kind of skeleton and a defense against predators. Janice told me that many sponges also protect themselves from grazing fish by using toxic chemicals, which might be useful in treating cancer, and that the taxonomy of Barrier Reef sponges is poorly known. I listened attentively because she was the researcher I would be working with.

The next day I went out with her on a little speedboat called Gemini to do sponge transplants at a depth of twenty feet for two and a half hours. We were doing the transplanting to see if the sponges would survive in different environments. It would have been dull work but I was on the Great Reef and was catching glimpses of marine life I'd never seen before. Most striking were the Crown of Thorns starfish and the giant sweet-lipped clams. Janice also pointed out a surprising number of sponge species. Some were encrusting sponges, others were vaselike, or finger-shaped, and many were amorphous. They ranged in color from bright orange to dull red, banana yellow to sky-blue. One delicate species was nearly transparent. Their oscula, or holes, varied in size and number. Their texture was smooth, or crinkled or prickly depending on the species, and each had a niche, a way of living, that was little understood. By the end of that dive I had come to share Dr. Thompson's fascination with Poriferians.

For the next eleven days I was at loose ends because Janice was busy with lab work. I latched onto Dr. Barnes for two days and helped him do a photographic survey of corals on Orpheus Reef and Falcon Reef. The forty-five foot, thirty-ton Sirius was our vessel for this short cruise, and there were only Barnes, Hardman, the Sirius's skipper and myself aboard. The weather was rough and I felt seasick much of the time. During our transit from Orpheus to Falcon Reef, Dr. Barnes and I had a long talk that helped calm my stomach. Among other things we talked about the relative merits of doing scientific research and teaching science. I told him I thought the work he and others like him were doing was extremely important. Barnes, one of the preeminent marine biologists of our time, pooh-poohed me.

"It's what you're doing that makes a difference," he said with sincerity. "My research doesn't mean a thing if the population at large can't understand, appreciate and act on it. You've got the harder and more important job."

I frittered away the rest of those eleven days in Townsville, a city of thirty thousand people that had a frontier feel. Two roads transected it: one, the coastal road, ran north south, the other road connected Townsville with the outback, and quaintly named places like Barabon, Nonda, Kajabbi, Boonderoo, and Utopia. Once in a while I would see a four-wheel drive vehicle covered with dust that had just come in from one of these towns, and if I could I'd strike up a conversation with its driver. At other times I walked the streets, sought out cheap restaurants, drank Foster's beer at the pubs, chased after sheilahs (Australian women) and worked out. This is how I got my nickname, "Bionic Bruce." On her way to work one of the secretaries at the institute encountered me as I was running up Townsville Mountain. The road was long and steep, and the woman reported that I had been racing up it like Lee Majors in "The Six Million Dollar Man" TV series, popular in Australia at the time. When the eleven days were up and I returned to the institute, Janice greeted me with, "How ya doing, Bionic?"

I spent the next four days with Janice aboard the Sirius, anchored at Rib Reef, transplanting hundreds of sponges and doing inventories. I learned more about sponges and I learned more about Janice. In addition to being very bright, Janice was attractive and personable. Unfortunately, she was already married to a bloke who looked a lot like me and who happened to be a landscape architect. He was the kind of husband Janice needed; he was always ready to quit whatever job he had and follow her to the Red Sea, or the Great Barrier Reef or anywhere else her research took her. Still, there was chemistry between us. Married or not she was exactly the kind of woman who appealed to me, and she had a thing for "bionic" men.

As we cruised back to Cape Cleveland from Rib Reef, Janice told me about our next voyage. We were going to distant Flinders Reef aboard the pride of the institute's fleet, the Harry Messel. Harry Messel was seventy feet long, weighed a hundred and seven tons and could make nine knots. She carried a crew of four and had six additional berths for researchers. She was a true ocean-going vessel, and had just returned from duty off the coast of Papua New Guinea. Our trip to Flinders would be a major expedition, led by Janice's boss, Dr. Clive Wilkinsen. We would gather data on sponges and coral, and collect liver samples from sharks we would catch with hook and line. Images of the movie *Blue Water, White Death* that Mike and I had seen years before surfaced in my mind, and I thrilled at the prospect of fulfilling a boyhood dream.

Everyone aboard Harry Messel was in a good mood when we set sail for Flinders reef a week later. Flinders was a jewel far out in the Coral Sea and was a favorite study site because of its crystal-clear water and pristine condition. Even the weather, usually stormy this time of year, was beautifully calm. By noon we had navigated through the shallow and treacherous barrier reef via Magnetic Island Passage and were in the open sea. Gentle swells broke against the bow and for a while a pod of playful porpoises escorted us through their realm. I watched them rainbow in and out of the ocean with pleasure and drank in the unspoiled salt air.

It is for such transcendent moments as this that we live, I thought, feeling pure, detached from myself and at one with the purple sea and the Harry Messel. *All the rest of it, the day to day trivia of eating, pissing, working, paying bills, and accumulating wealth, is just a distraction, an illusion.*

It was dark by the time we closed in on Flinders, and I had joined the Captain and Clive in the wheelhouse. The stars were out and the ocean was flat as glass. The Messel sliced through it effortlessly as we three traded stories in the dim light of the illuminated instruments. Clive told us about his experience with a monster-sized grouper whose territory he had violated while diving in a remote spot off the West Coast of Australia. He said the grouper had come out from behind a rocky outcrop, making grunting noises and working its Clive-sized mouth open and shut as it swam alongside him all the way to his skiff. Then he told us how the deadly, venomous sea snakes of the Coral Sea would swarm around a diver during mating season, and how one had to be careful to not provoke them into biting as they wound around the one's extremities.

The Captain, a weather-beaten man who spoke in a deep Australian brogue, told us that snakes were nothing, saltwater crocodiles were the beasts to watch out for. His brother had hired out to hunt them in New Guinea where every now and then a big croc would acquire the annoying habit of capsizing the canoes of native villagers and eating their occupants. He would tie a goat to a tree on the beach and wait for the killer to come for it, then shoot it from the safety of his tree stand. The Captain then told us that a few years ago the son of the AIMS director had been taken by a croc right below the Messel during a night dive in a New Guinea bay.

"But box jellyfish kill more people than sharks, snakes and salt water crocodiles put together," Dr. Wilkinsen said, and went on to explain how dangerous the young Medusas were when masses of them migrated out of the mangrove estuaries every summer. They were transparent and impossible to see, and once you were entangled in their stinging tentacles an agonizing death was sure to follow.

On that note I turned in for the evening, and when I awoke the next morning we were anchored on Flinders reef. The reef was a complex of corals that surrounded a low-lying sandbar about the size of a football field, which had on it a fifteen-foot high, unmanned weather station that sea birds perched on and decorated with excrement. The only other relief on the sandbar was a big, worm-riddled log that had been stranded above the water line. When we rolled the log over, hundreds of terrestrial hermit crabs were disturbed. How they got to the island I didn't have a clue. They seemed to be the only life present, except for sea birds like the blue-footed boobies, which made the most interesting nests out of the odd debris that washed up on the island. Their nests were a bizarre composite of coconut rinds, dried-up fish, lobster exoskeletons, shells, bits of sponge, somebody's lost sandal, a plastic toothbrush, bird skulls, tangled fishing line, small dehydrated starfish, and shark egg cases.

The reef itself was an underwater wilderness patrolled by numerous and bold five-foot barracuda, and big silver-tipped reef sharks that rarely encountered divers. Large schools of fish abounded, swimming in and around branching elkhorn corals, and distant rays could be seen gliding through the pellucid water. The place had a tense feel, as though the serenity of the moment could be splintered by an explosion of violence at any time, a feel that there was no real security here. Flinders reef, I analogized, was no different from the wild African savannas, where life-and-death struggles lurked just beneath a placid surface, where predators stalked their prey with cunning and patience, striking when least expected and devouring their victims with savage appetite.

Our first two days of diving consisted of doing sponge transplants at a depth of five feet on a sandy bottom adorned with sea fans and sea whips. These dives would last three hours and we'd come out of the water exhausted and cold, ready for a hot shower and the good meals the ship's cook always had waiting. On the third day we went to the reef wall and did a sponge survey at forty-five feet. As we moved along the wall collecting our specimens, a dozen or so silver-tipped reef sharks investigated us. I, holding the big plastic bag that Clive was filling with the sponges he was scraping off the wall, was keenly aware of their unfriendly presence. Clive was absorbed in his work. A shadow passed over us and the hair on the back of my neck would have stood up if it could have. I looked up to see the tail end of a ten-footer just above our heads. I tapped Clive and pointed to the shark. He gave it a glance and returned to his sponges. Janice and Hardman were ignoring the sharks as well.

I wasn't phobic about sharks, but these guys looked aggressive and I kept turning around to keep track of them. Toward the end of our dive I was looking around for the nth time when I saw the torpedo shape of one of the sharks heading straight for us at attack speed. I spun, bag in hand, hoping I could maneuver it between the shark and us in time, perfectly willing to sacrifice Clive's sponges to the jaws of our attacker. The big, fearsome animal veered off at the last possible second, and never returned. A few minutes later we concluded our transect and surfaced to the waiting Zodiac.

We surveyed the same wall at a depth of sixty feet the next day, and the sharks, having determined that we weren't food, let us be. Many of the sponges at this depth were different from those we had collected in shallower water. Janice, with whom I was teamed up this day, scrutinized some of them closely before putting them in my bag. They were new to science, perhaps, or a rare species or one she didn't expect to find at this depth. When we returned to the Harry Messel she sorted through them as if they were gold coins brought up from a Spanish Galleon.

We celebrated July 4th by doing a survey at sixty-five feet, and some more transplanting at five feet. The cook made a concession to Janice's and my holiday by cooking hamburgers for supper. The next day our all-too-brief exploration of Flinders reef came to an end. We weighed anchor and made for Rib Reef. There we spent a week transplanting sponges and taking liver samples from the small sharks Hardman would catch at night. The liver, which can make up as much as a third of a shark's weight, was sometimes infested with nasty, inch-long parasitic isopods.

The weather suddenly turned bad on the day we departed Rib Reef. When we anchored at Pandora Reef the next day, Harry Messel was rolling giddily and I was getting sick. It was on this day that my regulator chose to disappear. Hardman, who wasn't going down on the dive, loaned me his regulator, and I got in the water as soon as I could to get beneath the wave action where it was calm. But we only went down fifteen feet, and were buffeted by surge as we worked. I struggled not to vomit into my friend's regulator. I tried to concentrate on the sponges, to focus on anything but my roiling stomach, but it was no good. I regurgitated my breakfast through the mouthpiece of Hardman's regulator and out its exhaust ports, much to the delight of the tiny reef fish who made a feast of my gift to them.

When we surfaced, the Messel's crew was making preparations for a hasty departure. A gale warning had just been received. As soon as the divers got aboard, the anchor was winched up and we headed for Cape Cleveland. By afternoon we were battering our way through twenty-five foot seas. The Messel would rise in the air and crash down into waves that inundated her forward superstructure. I was in the wheelhouse with the Captain and Janice, and was reassured by the calm and confident manner in which our master steered us into each mountain of water. But I was sick again, and endangered my life by deserting the shelter of the bridge and pulling myself along a railing to the stern. There I held tightly to a post, and threw up to my heart's content where, at intervals, a foot of water would wash over the deck and carry away my vomit.

We made Cape Cleveland before dark and were glad of it. Nobody wanted to be out in twenty-five foot seas in the dark. Later we heard about a prawn trawler that was sunk in the gale not more than fifteen miles from us. The three crew persons had survived the sinking, but two of the three were taken by a fourteen foot tiger shark that showed up for breakfast on the first morning they were in the water, and for dinner the next night. It was closing in on the last survivor when a search helicopter rescued him.

I was given a twenty-day layoff, and decided to take a trip up the coast to Cape Tribulation, the isolated headland where Captain Cook had been shipwrecked. I caught a train north that took me through pine and eucalyptus forest to Cairns, a small city full of robust characters and mud-spattered jeeps. It was more tropical here than in Townsville, and a crocodile-filled river flowed through town. I was told rather offhandedly that when the river had overflowed into the streets a few weeks before, a "little six-footer" had seized a drunkard as he was walking home and nearly dragged him to his death. A cab driver had come to the rescue in the nick of time. This kind of stuff was always happening in these parts, and was hardly worth mentioning.

I liked Cairns and stayed there about a week. Then I caught a twelve-person bus to Daintree River National Park. We drove on a paved road lined with sugar cane plantations until we came to the Daintree River. There we crossed the river on an archaic, two-vehicle ferry that noisily belched black smoke, and we entered another world.

The road we now traveled was of red clay made slippery by recent rains, and bordered by luxuriant plant growth. We were in a coastal mountain rainforest, dissected by numerous streamlets running to the sea. Some of the streams along our way were bridged, others the doughty bus driver forded. Our progress slowed to a crawl as the road gradually got worse. At its end three backpackers and I were deposited at a rustic camp in the national park. I was lucky enough to procure a room with a bunk there, and slept soundly to a serenade of forest sounds that first night.

The next day the backpackers set out to Cape Tribulation. I decided on a weeklong stay at the camp and began my exploration of the surrounding forest. Tall hardwood trees, some of which had rocket-like fins at their bases, dominated it. These fins, I learned, were called buttresses, and kept the trees from blowing over in the wind. This was necessary because the trees had shallow root systems as a result of the poor soil. Instead of growing downward, the roots of these trees spread out just beneath the ground's surface, where they absorbed the nutrients from decaying leaves and branches.

I found my walks through the forest easy because there very little vegetation grew beneath these trees. Light was in short supply here, so many herbaceous plants had evolved an arboreal lifestyle, living as epiphytes in the tree tops or growing from the forest floor as vines. Some trees discouraged vine growth, though; their bark peeled off in thin sheets, so they were always free of hangers-on. Other trees start out their lives as epiphytes.

The Strangler Fig has a fascinating way of doing this. An adult fig tree attracts vectors with its fruit. These vectors-birds, bats and mammals, eat the fruit, which contains a laxative so its seeds pass quickly through their guts — and then disperse the seeds throughout the forest. When a seed lands in the crotch of a tree it germinates, sends roots down to the ground and eventually strangles its host. Strangler Figs belong to a genus with more than nine hundred species worldwide, and each species depends on a particular species of wasp to pollinate its flowers. A biologist doing research at the camp explained all this to me.

He also told me about the logging that was threatening the forest outside and inside the park. The wood from the trees was fine grained, handsome, dense and decay-resistant, and therefore very valuable. The problem was that once the trees were cut down on a large scale the entire rainforest ecosystem would unravel. The animals and insects that had co-evolved with the trees, and the rich community of fungi, molds and bacteria that decayed the vegetation on the forest floor, would be destroyed when the forest was leveled. Without them the trees could not make a comeback, and where once stood a green forest, there now grew only weedy pioneer plants living in an impoverished soil subject to severe erosion during the rainy season.

"We're not even certain how old they are," he concluded, considering a hundred and fifty-foot giant towering over the camp. "They don't have growth rings like trees in temperate zones. For all we know this tree could be a thousand years old."

On my return trip to Cairns I picked up some literature produced by a conservation society trying to save the Daintree Watershed, and read more about confrontation between loggers and environmentalists. But I was soon back aboard the Harry Messel and immersed in sponge research again.

The weather was marginal for my second cruise on the Messel, and I alternated between feeling sick and feeling okay. For a week we measured sedimentation rates and conducted ultraviolet radiation experiments at Davies Reef. Then we returned to port, and my volunteer work with AIMS came to an end. Janice threw a farewell party for me where I met her husband for the first time. I couldn't help liking him, and I knew as I hugged Janice goodbye that I would never see her again. "Take care of yourself, Bionic," she said as I turned to go.

"You too, Dr. Thompson," I retorted.

The Leaders of the International Children's Rainforest Network in Cambridge, England. Left to right: Mineohara-Kogen Suzaka, the author, Eha Kern, Bernd Kern, Daniel Hub, the group's guide, and Robin Jollife.

CHAPTER TWENTY

THE SINISTER MINISTER?

Erosion and flooding in rainforest watersheds that have been deforested cause thousands of deaths and billions of dollars of damage annually.
— Save the Rainforest fact sheet

When I returned to Dodgeville I found out that I hadn't missed out on the Self-Help Housing project after all. Delays of one sort or another had postponed construction, and in September I joined six families in the building of our houses on Jamie Street. The project worked like a barn raising. Every weekend we would work collectively on one or two of the seven houses being built. The pouring of foundations, the plumbing and electrical wiring were contracted out, but we did the rest. By Easter we were living in snug, albeit identical homes.

It was while my house still had that smell of newness and fresh paint that I met my second cousin, Linda, at a family reunion in Wisconsin Rapids. She was Aunt Daisy's granddaughter, and a real sweetheart. We had a love affair that really heated up when she flew to Alaska for a weekend to visit me after I had temporarily suspended our lovemaking to go visit Greg. When I returned to Dodgeville in late June I got into a routine of driving to Chicago every weekend to see Linda, or hosting her visits. She loved to come up and play with the two puppies I had adopted, Ajax and Paris. For my birthday she gave me a jersey of one of the players on the Chicago Blackhawks, and got us tickets to see the Green Bay Packers-Chicago Bears game at Lambeau Field. The Bears won the game 9 to 7. That was the year they went on to win the Super Bowl. Linda split up with me after this game, not because she was a Bears fan and I was now a Packer backer, but because we were cousins. She wanted children, and even though the doctor said it was okay for second cousins to have children she wasn't comfortable with the idea.

Years after Linda and I broke up, the jersey she gave me caused some trouble. One night I wore it to a seedy bar in Tucson, Arizona. I masqueraded as the real kick-ass hockey player whose name was on the jersey. I thought I was dying because I had discovered a lump underneath my arm while sunning myself the day before in a streambed that ran through the property of a remote ranch that Steve, who I was visiting, was overseeing. There were some mean-looking characters in the bar. The biggest and most surly was the ex-husband of a flirtatious woman who'd asked me to dance with her because she had heard my drunken boasting about my old days as a hockey player when I used to brawl every night in the rink. As we danced she pointed out her ex, who was glaring at us from his barstool.

"He's as jealous as sin," she complained. "No one will go out with me because they're afraid of him."

I held her tighter and told her after what I had been through playing hockey her ex was about as frightening to me as a furry bunny. The ex, observing my hands slipping down to his former wife's nether regions, got off his barstool, swaggered over and planted himself in front of me with his arms folded.

"What's your problem?" I asked him.

"That's my wife you're dancing with."

"So what?" I rejoined, not caring whether she had lied to me about their being divorced or not, and hoping to provoke him further.

"You want to get the crap beat out of you?" he asked with a scowl.

Feeling like I was in Jim Croce's song, *Bad Bad Leroy Brown*, I laughed in his face and said, "I'd like to see you try, you pathetic sack of crap."

He turned purple with rage, but he'd heard me talking about my hockey days too, and he went back to his barstool sputtering some nonsense about the shotgun he had in the trunk of his car and how he was going to blow my head off with it.

Aroused by this exchange, his wife, or ex-wife, asked me to go home with her and we headed out. Her ex was waiting in the shadows for us and I comforted myself with the thought that I wouldn't end my days lying in a hospital bed being eaten away by cancer. But the shotgun was still in his trunk, and instead of shooting me he started to argue with the love of his life. She called him a bastard at some point, whereupon he took her by the blouse and flung her to the ground. The blouse remained in his hand, and the woman, breasts popping out of her bra, sat crying on the parking lot pavement. Seething with anger he next grabbed my collar with both his hands. I countered by gripping his wrists.

"Now it's your turn!" he prophesied.

It wasn't. I lived up to the name on the back of my jersey, threw a punch into his big fat belly, and another into his jaw. He crumbled at my feet and clutched my knees as I beat him on the back. By this time a crowd was gathering, and I played my role to the hilt by importuning them to pull me off of the man and exclaiming, "I've killed in the rink and I'll kill again." I half believed it myself.

Two guys separated me from my fallen foe and told me to skedaddle before the police came. As I did I looked over my shoulder to see my little divorcee bending over her ex husband, kissing his cheek and making up with him. A few days later I went to the doctor and learned that my lump was a harmless knot of fat.

After my breakup with Linda, which coincided with the death of Ajax, I had a little time to help Barb with the building of her Self-Help home in nearby Barneveld. I had talked her into joining the program. We completed her house in the spring, and she gave a housewarming that was attended primarily by Shake Rag'ers. I dusted off my play for the party; we did a reading, and it was decided that we would perform it in the fall.

I spent the intervening summer going door to door on behalf of Wisconsin's Environmental Decade, trying to convince people to join the organization and the fight to stop urban sprawl, reduce acid rain–causing pollution and minimize the logging of state forest land. I was pretty good at this because I really believed in what I was telling people and believed that what I was doing was making a difference.

In August I resumed my teaching duties and in September we had the tryouts for *Sinister Minister?* I was director, and I picked

Roland to be Matthew, the protagonist, Tom Kelly to be Squire Fuddy, and Dick to be the evil Millhouse Mason. We began rehearsals, and as the play came together I sensed that it was going to be a success. Still, I was very nervous on opening night. Would the audience be able to follow the plot? Would Tom remember his lines? Would people laugh? Would my mother like it?

My doubts vanished when the first scene succeeded in setting up the story line and getting some giggles, and I knew I had a hit on my hands when the first act ended to thunderous applause. In the lobby people were buzzing about the play and laughing over the last scene, in which Matthew finally declares his love for Julia and kisses her just as the Squire walks into the house. Astonished, the Squire drops his gun and shoots himself in the foot.

Through the second and third acts I watched the play build to a climax. It was extremely gratifying to see my characters come to life onstage. To see Julia, my ideal woman, take form, and note the contrast between my better half, represented by Matthew, and the darker side of my personality, symbolized in Millhouse. To hear the audience laugh at all the silly words I put into the squire's mouth, and to observe their rapt attention to Ann's final speech, which resolved everything and allowed for a happy ending. I was congratulated after the play but felt an emptiness after the final performance.

This emptiness was compounded by the death of Paris, who had been hit by a car during the production of *Sinister Minister?* The police had found his frozen corpse along the highway and called me so I could retrieve him. I stored Paris in my garage during our last show, a Sunday matinee, and after the cast party at my house I asked Tom if he would help me inter my pet. Tom looked at me with surprise, for I had kept Paris' death a secret until everyone else had left so as not to spoil the festivities, then he said, "Oh, I'm sorry, of course I will."

We went into the garage, where Tom grabbed the shovel and I took up Paris in my arms. A bitter wind blew the snow of a December storm into our faces as we walked to the bend in the creek where I planned to entomb Paris. I tried to be brave but the smell of Paris' fur brought back memories of how I had loved him. I buried my face in his coat and began to sob. Tom didn't say a word, he just continued to walk along beside me. When we got to the creek I set Paris down, took the shovel from Tom and began to chip away at the concrete-hard earth. It took quite a while to break through the frost, and I'm sure Tom was freezing in the light jacket he was wearing. But he stood by me in the windy, snowy night without complaint, and after I had placed Paris in his grave and covered him with the black dirt of the creek-bottom, my Squire Fuddy put his arm around his playwright's shoulder and walked him home.

A Jaguar in Belize

CHAPTER TWENTY-ONE

ROXANNE

Global temperatures have risen by 1.2 degrees Fahrenheit since 1860.
This has occurred because humans have pumped billions
of tons of carbon dioxide, a greenhouse gas, into the atmosphere.
— World Watch Institute fact sheet

Roxanne had built a house in Barneveld through the same Self-help program as Barb, and had played a bit part in *Sinister Minister?* She had a boyfriend named Tony who owned a company called Al's Sewer. He pumped out people's septic tanks for a living. Roxanne had hinted to me during the play that she was getting ready to break up with him. I hurried things along by inviting her on a weekend skiing trip to La Crosse. She accepted.

I fell in love with Roxanne before I knew what was happening. She was good-looking, extroverted and athletic, and to the casual onlooker a woman with every thing going for her. But what made me love her was her vulnerability. Behind her gay exterior a troubled little girl struggled with feelings of inadequacy. Her self-esteem was so low at times that she would comfort herself by bingeing on junk food and then throwing up. She was deeply ashamed of this behavior, and only told me about it because she had fallen in love with me, too. I, in turn, told her about my manic depressive disorder, and how I had nearly committed suicide in Mike's garage. This sharing of our dark secrets brought us even closer.

Roxanne thought *Sinister Minister?* was a great play and idolized me for it. When I won the Wisconsin Playwright of the Year award she was as thrilled about the honor as I was. At the award

banquet she squeezed my hand with pride as the master of cer-
emonies read the judge's critique:

"First Place awarded to Bruce Calhoun for *The Sinister Minister?* This is an amazing, almost magical tour de force of playwriting.
Each character is a marvelous opportunity for a skilled actor to
do something powerful, original and exciting. The dialogue is
crisp, succinct and extremely well controlled. There is much pro-
foundly important social philosophy here. You're never preached
to, yet you will not leave the theatre without thinking some new
thoughts about your time and society. I hope the play will get the
top professional treatment if deserves."

As it turned out the play didn't get any professional treatment. I couldn't get it published or performed. I didn't really
care, though, because I had Roxanne, and our future looked
bright. We were both high-energy people who enjoyed being
active and doing new things. But we enjoyed spending quiet
evenings together, too. We would cuddle up on the couch, read
our respective books, and keep each other's toes warm on cold
winter nights.

There was only one problem: Roxanne was still working as
Tony's secretary, and he kept pressuring her to come back to him.
It was very awkward for her to be around him, but she couldn't
afford to quit because he paid her so well, and she needed the
money to make the payments on her house and her new car.

We scanned the want ads looking for a job for her, and one
day I said, "Look at this. Wanted — outgoing, well organized,
energetic person with management experience to run office of
political campaign."

Roxanne shook her head and told me she didn't have the quali-
fications for the position.

"Sure you do," I encouraged. "You've been running Tony's
business for years."

With a little more prodding I got her to interview for the job,
and it was given to her. She was to be the office manager for Ann
Haney, the Republican congressional candidate from Wisconsin's
Second District. We were both ecstatic and went out to dinner to
celebrate. We talked about the new life opening up for her, and
for us. Summer was approaching and she told me I should rent
out my house and move in with her, and in the fall, after Ann

Haney had won the election — well, who knew what that could lead to?

So on June 5, 1986 I gave up my bachelor life, packed my clothes, handed the keys of my house to a retired couple who'd come up from Florida for the summer, and moved in with my Roxanne. The searching was over, the mistakes, the infatuations were behind me. Gene's sister, Gale, the two Nancys, Eleanor, the diplomat's daughter, the French singer, Carol of Calgary, Bernadette, Matar, Lynette, Marie, Dr. Thompson and Linda had been preludes, learning experiences, furnace fires that had forged me into the man Roxanne loved. It all made sense now, and I slept in the arms of my love that night the luckiest man in the world.

For the next month Roxanne would wake up on weekday mornings and cheerfully drive to her Madison office while I drove the other way to Governor Dodge Park, where I was employed as a summer naturalist. It was a dream job that Gari had helped me get. The two of us took park visitors to the beaver pond, the pioneer homestead, the Indian rock shelter, the cave, the waterfall, the fossil quarry and the springhouse. We also conducted canoe tours of the lake, and gave native prairie walks during which we explained the ecology of yellow-flowered compass plants, desert-like rattlesnake masters, six-foot tall Indian cup, Black-eyed Susans, little blue-stem grass and purple coneflowers.

One day I caught a seven-foot bull snake that had been sunning itself in the quarry, and showed it to the fossil-hunting children. They were afraid of it at first, but bull snakes are gentle and soon the children were standing in line to pet "the serpent." Another day I discovered a Great Horned Owl along the park road. It had been hit by a car and was dazed. I wrapped it in my shirt, took it back to the park office where it recovered its senses, and released it as a group of bystanders watched appreciatively. Then there were the white-tailed deer, wild turkeys and raccoons that people routinely saw on their walks with Gari and me. But the most interesting animals in the park were the beavers. While I was giving a slide show on them in our outdoor auditorium one evening, a representative of their kind felled an aspen that blocked the parking lot exit. That, and their building of lodges, damning of streams, which created wetlands, and plugging of culverts, which

caused flooding of park roads, made them deserving of our fascination.

On weekends Roxanne and I would go bicycling on an old
railroad bed that the Wisconsin Department of Resources had
converted into a bike trail. Where once the trains of a bygone
era had huffed and puffed their way to destinations named Blue
Mounds, Ridgeway and Black Earth, we toured beneath the
shadows of oaks and maples, and sped past the Queen Anne's
lace, angel parsnip, evening primrose and tall bluestem grass lining
the way. As the summer progressed, we did less of this and more
campaign stuff, like attending the frequent fundraisers for Ann
Haney.

Many of these events were held in Madison. They were mostly
parties where we smooched up to the affluent elite and listened
to their self-serving ideologies. By the third or fourth cocktail
politics usually gave way to discussions of real estate investments
and stock options. After that the flirting would commence, and
often Roxanne found it difficult to extricate herself from in-
creasingly personal conversations with potbellied businessmen
who were big supporters of Ann Haney. It all seemed pretty sleazy
to me. I'd been a Democrat my entire life, an admirer of Robert
Kennedy, Martin Luther King and George McGovern, men who
had tried to cure some of society's ills, and had stood for something above and beyond self-interest. Here I saw only greed, ar-
rogance and a lust for power. But Roxanne was my woman, and
for her sake I, too, was a big supporter of Ann Haney.

As the campaign heated up I saw less and less of Roxanne. She
had proved indispensable as an office manager and was a natural
at public relations. Ann began taking her to the county fairs, the
dairy breakfasts, the farmer's markets and the small town parades
that made up a politician's summer itinerary. When I did see
Roxanne she was usually exhausted from the frenetic life she was
leading. There was no more time for bike rides, or walks through
the countryside, or sunsets. There was hardly even time for
lovemaking, and the tantalizing references to marriage had been
dropped from her conversation. I began to press for attention, for
an acknowledgment that I was still an important part of her life.
This only drove Roxanne further from me. She told me I was
smothering her. Then she started staying over in Madison three

or four nights a week. I would get a call, or maybe I wouldn't, informing me that she'd been working late in the office again and would be sleeping at her parents' house.

Things went completely haywire the day I accompanied her to a parade in Boscobel. I hadn't seen or talked to her in nearly a week, and I wanted to communicate to her my concerns over what was happening. She was too busy to talk at the parade, so I bided my time and watched the procession. Ann Haney was in it, of course, and so was Bob Kastenmier, the man she was trying to unseat, Kastenmier had been in congress for twenty-four years. He was a man of integrity, and I had always voted for him in years past. He had known my stepfather Orla, and while a freshman congressman had attended Orla's funeral. As he passed and looked my way I had the oddest feeling that he recognized me, that he knew I was betraying him, and that he wasn't angry with me but rather worried about the path I was on. Maybe he gave that empathetic look to everyone, or maybe it was just my state of mind, but it gave me a premonition of disaster.

On our ride home I broached the subject of Roxanne's working too much and ignoring me. I said that I wanted her to come home at night, and find a way to make some time for us. She responded that she loved what she was doing, and that things would only get more hectic as the election neared. I countered that Ann Haney could get along without her one day a week.

"If it's a choice between you and my job," she said in a hard voice, "I'll take the job. I can always get another man." This bombshell obliterated me. I sat in the passenger seat of her Jetta, dumbstruck, bleeding, pierced to the heart. I was just another man to her, worse than that, an impediment, a nuisance that was distracting her from the campaign.

The week that followed was hell. She spent only two nights at home, one stuffing envelopes for her Ann Haney, another talking on the phone to a young and upcoming attorney she had met at a function. She talked about how exciting the campaign was, but also confided that she found her job difficult, that sometimes Ann was a bitch to be around, that so much was expected of her, and that the stress was almost too much. These were things, I thought, she should have been talking to me about, and I said something to that effect after she hung up.

"Scott understands what I'm going through," she responded, and I felt like strangling her right then and there. She must have seen in it my eyes because she didn't mention his name again, and made herself scarce the rest of the evening. The next morning she was gone before I woke up and I didn't hear from her for three days. Finally I got through to her at work and asked her when she was coming home. She told me she wasn't. She told me she was afraid of me, of what I might do.

I was feared now, and there was no hope for me. I wondered if I would ever see Roxanne again, and I looked at the calendar and saw that my house was rented out for two more weeks, and that I had one more week to go at the park. Somehow I managed to perform my duties there but I was absolutely wretched. I told Gari of my plight. There was little he could say, though. Nothing consoles scorned lovers. The future is a blank to them. The places they haven't seen, the people they haven't met, the roses they haven't smelled, the mountains they haven't climbed do not exist. There is only the dull throbbing in their hearts and the utter sense of loss at having been rejected by the one person on earth they can't live without.

It got worse when my summer employment at the park ended. I sat around Roxanne's house recalling precious moments, like the time she had interrupted our lovemaking on the living room carpet to shut the curtains. I dwelt on the candlelit dinner she had cooked the night I moved in, torturing myself by recounting the times she had told me she loved me *so* much, and second-guessing myself about the job I had found for her. When I could stand it no more I put on my jogging shoes and went for a run. It was a hot and humid August day and I wanted to punish my body, to suffer so much that the awful hurt in my heart would be drowned out by physical pain.

As I ran along the bike trail I decided to follow it all the way to Madison, thirty miles distant, or die of heat exhaustion in the attempt, which would put me out of a misery that seemed worse than death. The first ten miles were easy, too easy, and my mind continued to boil in anguish. But after twenty I began to feel the effects of dehydration and fatigue. This was what I wanted, the breaking down of the machine, the failure of its systems, the short-circuiting of its data processing banks, the dissolution of its being.

When I reached the outskirts of Madison it was growing dark, my endurance was ebbing and a terrible thirst afflicted me. But my marathon didn't end until I ran up to the A & W near Roxanne's parents' home. I quenched my thirst with four mugs of orange drink, and walked on rubbery legs to the house, my head splitting with pain. "Roxanne's not here," her sister said, looking at me as if I was a specter. "You can sleep on the sofa of the screened porch."

The next day, after I had caught a ride back to Barneveld, Roxanne phoned me and we had a long talk. I assured her I would never harm a hair on her head, and told her she should come home. That night she did, and three days later she accompanied me to my ten-year class reunion. She impressed all my male friends with her looks, and heaped praise upon me, telling everyone about *Sinister Minister?* We drank and danced, and made love when we got home. The following morning she told me she was pregnant, but not with my child. I thought of the period when our sex life had been disrupted, and of the phone call with Scott.

"It's Tony's," she said.

This I did not understand. Why discard me for a man she had wanted desperately to get away from, for a man who fit in with her new life style even less than I did? "It doesn't matter," I told her. "We'll get married and I'll raise it as my own."

"No," she replied. "I don't want to get married right now, and I don't want to have a child. I want to get an abortion. I need four hundred dollars."

So this was why she had called me, why we had gone to the reunion, why she had made love to me the night before. Or was it more complicated than that? Had she gone to bed with the septic-tank-emptier to assuage her feelings of low self-worth, and come back to me simply because I was someone who understood her and could be turned to in a crisis?

"I've been bingeing again, too," she admitted. "It's the pressure of this job."

I offered once more to marry her and raise her baby. She would have none of it, so I gave her the money and she went to a clinic the next day. For all I knew the baby she aborted was mine, or Scott's or who knows? As I lay in bed with her a few nights later, wanting only to cradle her in my arms she said, "I think you better start sleeping on the couch downstairs."

I knew I couldn't do this. I knew I couldn't be in the same house with her and not be her lover. It was better to end it cleanly and walk out the door like a man, giving her what she wanted and didn't want.

"No," I said. "If you don't want me in your bed I don't belong in your house." I got up, gathered my things, went back to the bed and said, "Goodbye Roxanne."

Her face was buried in her pillow, and she was weeping into it. But she didn't tell me to put my things down and come back to bed; she offered only a weak, muffled goodbye. I turned and walked out of her house, out of her life, and into the darkness of the night.

CHAPTER TWENTY-TWO

SAVE THE RAINFOREST, INC.

Fourteen of the hottest years on record have occurred since 1980. The hot temperatures have caused extreme droughts in some regions and unusually strong storms in others. In the first seven months of 1997, 72 billion dollars of damage was attributed to weather phenomena.
— World Watch Institute fact sheet

Bob Kastenmier thrashed Ann Haney in that November's election, and did so again two years later. After Haney's first drubbing, Roxanne married Tony, had a child by him, moved into a big stone house and started a wrecking company. I spiraled into another depression.

With my school insurance policy in hand I was admitted to the psychiatric ward of a Madison hospital and became the roommate of a smashed-up man who was only alive because the roof of a car had broken his fall. He didn't talk much; I was of little comfort to him as I sat looking out the window, paraphrasing Shakespeare. Life's but a poor player that struts and frets his hour upon the stage and then is heard no more. A tale told by an idiot, full of sound and fury, signifying nothing.

Gari picked me up when I was released after a week of therapy and drug treatment. I was tender for a long time. Cassandra helped. I had been smitten by her during a Christmas Eve party on Jim Quast's ranch, and had taken her home that night to fill the void left by the death of my dog, Paris. Sarah, too, was good for me. She was a lovely young teacher at Dodgeville Elementary. She had seen my play, heard my story, and thought of me as some kind of tragic figure. She gave me her companionship, and would have given me more, too, had I been ready to take it. But I wasn't.

By the time summer rolled around I was feeling better, and I wrote a play called *The Collection*. Dan Capps, who had displayed a multitude of insects at our elementary school, inspired the play. He had collected these insects all over the world, mostly in exotic rainforest locales where most of the planet's insects reside and where many species grow to staggering sizes. His walking sticks were among the largest and most bizarre of his specimens. Some were over a foot long, most were armored with fascinating patterns of defensive spikes, and all would have been nearly impossible to spot had they been in their forest home. They came from places like the Congo, Borneo, and the Amazon.

Dan's beetles represented a good portion of the four hundred thousand species found in that order of *Insecta*. There were tiny green and red iridescent beetles, golf ball–sized beetles with horns for jousting, beetles with mandibles that could embrace a man's thumb, and beetles with antennae twice the length of their bodies. Some were mounted with their shells open and their heavily veined wings spread. Others were displayed with carapace closed, looking like miniature Volkswagens.

The preying mantises in his collection were right out of a Hollywood horror film. They were alien-looking creatures with bulbous eyes and grasping, stiletto-armed forelegs. These predators would have given their prey nightmares if they had been capable of REM sleep.

His grasshoppers were fantastic, too. A few were the size of cigars, and they ranged from army green to bright yellow. There were so many different kinds that it made your head spin.

The butterflies and moths were my favorites, though. Their large, colorful wings were beautiful, and the examples of mimicry were endless. The largest of the butterflies, as big as dinner plates, were from New Guinea. The other butterflies were from rainforests in Central and South America, Southeast Asia and equatorial Africa.

As people wondered at his amazing insects collection Dan would tell them how they had been co-evolving with rainforest plants for millions of years. He explained how some were ruthless hunters, others useful pollinators, and still others leaf-eaters that plants had developed toxins to defend themselves against. This had been going on for so long that the leaves of many plants had become pharmaceutical warehouses, full of chemicals that had the potential to cure human diseases. But rainforests were being cut down so fast that many of these plants were going extinct, and with each extinction the chances lessened of discovering compounds that could defeat cancer, AIDS and other scourges of mankind.

I incorporated Dan's and my concern over rainforest destruction in *The Collection,* along with his fixation on insects. I also surrounded him with comical characters. His best friend was an insect exterminator who worked for Bugkill and believed that "the only good insect is a dead insect." His wife and her best friend were tabloid junkies who believed in everything from the fountain of youth to reincarnation and the alien presence of Melodians. His benefactor was a bumbling millionaire who wanted to own the biggest insect collection in the world but couldn't tell the difference between a katydid and a cicada.

The Collection was a hit in Mineral Point, but like *Sinister Minister?* it failed to interest publishers. I refocused on teaching, and began to chum around with Juan, our exchange teacher from Costa Rica. He had a wife and two kids back home, and asked me about my family. When I told him I wasn't married he was shocked and he told me I should come down and visit him in Costa Rica where there was no shortage of beautiful women who would want to raise a family with a man like me. I didn't take him seriously at first, but by summer I had decided to give Costa Rica a try.

Juan met me at the airport in San Jose and took me on an eight-hour bus ride — during which we had to stand in the aisle most of the time — to the little town of Cuidad Cortes, where he lived and worked. I lived with Juan and his family as a pampered guest for a month. I was always given the biggest plate of rice and beans and the tallest glass of fruit juice for dinner. For breakfast I was often the only one to enjoy an egg with the bread that was bought fresh from the corner *paneria.*

Juan's matchmaking left something to be desired. The girls he introduced me to ranged from sixteen to eighteen years old, far too young for me to consider marrying. I told this to Juan.

"But girls marry young here," he explained.

I countered that I was looking for a wife, not a daughter. This sobered him. Then he brightened and said we would go back to San Jose and find a woman for me there.

I put myself in his hands. We took the long bus ride back to San Jose, over a spine of mountains, down a river valley and into Costa Rica's capital. This time we had a seat and I was able to see the rugged landscape we drove through. Where the forest remained, it was achingly beautiful. Where the trees had been cut down, cows grazed in degraded pastures, and rainwater carved ugly gullies down hillsides.

In San Jose, with Juan's assistance, I met and wooed Marisol. She was a very sweet young woman who was in the mood to get married, too. I bought her an engagement ring and took her on a sightseeing vacation of her country. First we went to the ocean, where I almost broke my neck body surfing when a big wave caught me, arched my back and drove me face first into the sand beach with tremendous force. All I suffered, however, was a bloody nose, which Marisol tended to.

Next we caught a bus to Monteverde. An hour into the ride the bus turned off the main highway and started up the mountain on a rough gravel road. There were numerous *fincas* along our way. Some of these farms were still partially forested, some were planted with fruit trees, but most were barren-looking properties that had coarse grasses growing up around tree stumps, and a few scraggly head of cattle making their way up and down steep, eroded slopes. It wasn't until we reached the community of Monteverde that the scenery improved.

We checked into a very nice mountain lodge, and the next day took a hike through the Monteverde Cloud Forest Reserve. This was a cool, damp and lush forest that the Monteverde community, mostly Quakers who had left the United States to escape military service, had set aside as a reserve in order to protect their watershed. The mountaintop forest was home to the resplendent quetzal, a holy bird of the Mayans, the tiny, yellow-eyelash viper that could fit into your palm, sloths, monkeys, bellbirds and many other creatures. Marisol and I saw several different species of hummingbirds feeding on the nectar of flowers at the welcoming center, but saw few other signs of animal life in the reserve. This lack of animal sightings by visitors was typical. The rainforest is a great place for animals to hide and most are shy around strangers.

We did hear a host of animal sounds, however, and pondered many interesting plants, and I was keen on returning to the reserve again the next day.

When we got back to the lodge the owner told us about a slide show on the natural history of Monteverde that would be given in the lobby after dinner, so after the repast Marisol and I joined some other tourists for the presentation.

Our speaker introduced himself as a biologist who was doing research in the area, then turned off the lights and began to project some astounding images on the movie screen of the animals Marisol and I had failed to see during our foray in the reserve. There were close-up shots of spider and howler monkeys, anteaters, peccaries, albino fruit bats, leaf-cutter ants, harpy eagles, ring-tailed coatimundi, ocelots, and jaguars.

As one slide followed another the speaker shared with us his knowledge of these animals and their ecology. He told us that ants are the true rulers of the rainforest, the accumulated mass of their bodies outweighing the biomass of any other animal life form. There are countless variations of them, from the solitary, one-inch forager ant to the acacia ants that made their homes in the hollow thorns of the tree, drinking of its nectar in return for protecting its juicy leaves from caterpillars, and snipping away deadly climbing vines.

He went on to say that when it comes to mammals bats take the cake. There are over nine hundred species worldwide, and there are as many species of bats in Costa Rica as there are all other kinds of mammals combined. There are fruit bats, insect-eating bats, nectar-feeding bats, frog-catching bats and vampire bats. Their role in the rainforest was pollination and seed-dispersion.

At this point Marisol yawned and excused herself. She didn't speak much English and had become bored. I stayed to hear about the golden toad that had evolved in isolation on Monteverde's mountaintop, and about *Penas Blancas* — the name given to the forest on Monteverde's eastern slope and the river valley that drained it. Unlike the western slope that we had driven up, it was still in a pristine state. But that would change soon unless action was taken, because farmers were beginning to purchase acreage from the land speculators who held title to this forest. The

Monteverde Conservation League had been formed to purchase this land before the farmers did, and save it from destruction. "Would anybody like to make a contribution to the league?" he concluded.

I emptied my pocket of its thirteen dollars, gave the money to the biologist and told him I would be right back. I went up to our room, ferreted out another twenty-five dollars and returned to the lobby where I added it to my donation.

A few days later Marisol and I returned to San Jose where I initiated a discussion that led to the cancellation of our plans. She was heartbroken and in tears at the airport where she returned the engagement ring. On the plane ride home I felt very bad about disappointing her, but she was not the soul mate I had been looking for, and it had been better to admit my mistake early rather than late.

I was also troubled by the deforestation I had seen in her country, and the bus shuttle ride from Chicago to Madison reminded me of the global implications of cutting down the rainforest. As I looked at the windows I saw parched cornfields that were suffering from a record-setting drought, and remembered how the biologist in Monteverde had warned that cutting down and burning rainforests was adding carbon dioxide, a greenhouse gas, to the atmosphere, and exacerbating global warming.

The beginning of another school year distracted me for awhile. But one day, after showing my own slides of the rainforest to students, I expressed to my office-mate, Jack Harrison, what a shame it was that rainforests were being wiped out, and that the students I was teaching would probably never have the chance to visit them as I had. Jack agreed with me, saying, "It doesn't make sense to teach kids science and preach about ecology while we let the world go to pot on them."

Jack's comment fermented in my brain that night, and the next morning I had a "Eureka" moment. Why not start our own student / teacher organization to save rainforests? There had to be a lot of biology teachers out there who felt as I did, who cared about the environment and had heard that rainforests were being destroyed at the rate of one acre per second, and that this would have dire consequences. What if we all joined together and offered our students a chance to take action, to get involved in issues that would affect the quality of the world they, and their children and their children's children would be living in?

I discussed the idea with Jack and Gari; they were all for it. The first step was to come up with a plan of action, a campaign that schools around the country could undertake. I decided that we could circulate a petition. We would ask the World Bank to stop funding dams that flooded rainforests, to refuse incentive loans to cattle ranchers for clearing land, and to stop supporting road-building in the Amazon, which promoted settlement in areas where a forest complex thrived but the soil was too poor to sustain farming. There was also a place on the petition where people could put down the amount of money they wanted to donate to the Monteverde Conservation League to help buy the endangered forest of Penas Blancas.

The next step was to test out the petition. I rounded up a score of student volunteers and we hit the pavement in Dodgeville, going door to door as I had for Wisconsin's Environmental Decade. We succeeded in gathering over three hundred signatures and raising three hundred and twenty-three dollars. If our success could be replicated by the other thirty thousand high schools in the United States, the world's rainforests could be given a much better prognosis.

So I went on to step three, crafting a letter on our school stationary, inviting my fellow teachers to take up the cause with us. Gari and Jack reviewed the letter, then I drove the two hundred and fifty miles to Ashland to ask Rob's and Dorothy's opinion of not only the letter but also the whole concept. Being experienced at this sort of thing they helped me fine-tune the letter, and said I should apply to the IRS to establish my organization as a nonprofit charity.

Step four consisted of filling out the IRS forms with the help of Bill Dyke, a Shake Rag'er who was an attorney, the former mayor of Madison, and the father of girl I liked but could never get to first base with. After this I acquired the names and addresses of all the biology teachers in Dane County. With Jack's computer and his help I set up a program that merged the first name of each teacher with the letter. We printed out about fifty letters, mailed them out and waited for a response. About 40 percent of the teachers wrote back and said they wanted to join in with us. We sent them copies of the petition and commenced step six, the mailing of the letter to the rest of the country's thirty thousand biology teachers.

This is where things got very expensive. First we had to buy the name lists and address tags from educational marketing companies. Then we needed thirty thousand envelopes and sheets of letterhead, plus thirty thousand stamps. I paid for the addresses out of my own pocket. The envelopes and letterhead were printed gratis by John Bass's Park Printing House of Verona. Most of the stamps were purchased with my savings; Jack chipped in the remaining five hundred dollars.

Next we had to deal with our administration, or not deal with it. Our new district administrator was no Monte Hottman, and I guessed that he would find some reason to object to our crusade. We ended up not telling anyone what we were doing, hoping that all would be forgiven after we had saved the world.

Lastly the thirty thousand names had to be entered into Jack's computer so they could be merged with the letter, after which the letters had to be printed, signed, folded and stuffed into envelopes. Then the mailing labels and stamps had to be stuck on the envelopes. We wore out Jack's printer producing the letters, my hand signing the letters, and my students' zeal doing the busy work. It was a daunting undertaking but we accomplished it by spring, and in March we received notice from the IRS that our status as a tax-exempt, nonprofit environmental organization had been approved. I looked at the letter with satisfaction, and thought of the saying, "Life is something that happens to you while you're making other plans." I had gone to Costa Rica seeking a woman, and instead had come home to found SAVE THE RAINFOREST, INC. (STR).

CHAPTER TWENTY-THREE

HAPPY BIRTHDAY

In 1998 an iceberg larger than the state of Delaware broke off the Antarctic ice sheet. Scientists fear this could be the beginning of a massive meltdown that will cause sea levels to rise by five meters.
— World Watch Institute fact sheet

In May I took a break from *Save the Rainforest, Inc.* to go on a canoe trip in northern Wisconsin with Roland, Jeff, Rob, Rob's brother Nate and a journalist friend of Rob's. Jeff drove up to Dodgeville from O'Fallon, Illinois, and he, Roland and I continued on from there, joining the others in Rob's cottage near Ashland. Rob informed us that the Brule was running high, that the water was ice cold and that it would be dangerous to canoe the river right now. So we altered our plans and decided to go canoeing on a nearby lake and try our luck at fishing.

We arrived at the lake early the next morning and launched our respective canoes into the water. Roland embarked with Jeff, while Rob and the journalist teamed up in the second canoe, and Nate and I manned the third. As we paddled out into the lake I remarked to Nate that our canoe seemed unstable. He agreed with me, and we both took care to watch our balance. We didn't want to topple into the freezing lake water, which still had some thin sheets of ice floating in its middle.

At first we all stayed close to each other, but after a while we fanned out in search of a "good hole." Nate and I ended up in the middle of the lake, between the other canoes, separated from each by a couple of hundred feet. About a half-hour later we heard Rob shout, and turned to see him and the journalist tipping over in their canoe. It seemed to happen in slow motion, and for a moment it looked comical. But this was no joke. The temperature of the water was at most thirty-six degrees, and our two companions would not last long in such cold water. Nate and I didn't even bother to reel in our lines. We grabbed our paddles and stroked like the devil to reach Rob and his friend in time.

As we approached them I worried that in their panic they would try to hoist themselves into our canoe, and tip us over as well. That would have surely resulted in some deaths, as Roland and Jeff, who were also paddling like crazy to reach the scene, would never have been able to rescue all four of us. From a distance of ten feet I yelled at the two men to remain calm, that we would get them to shore somehow. Rob nodded his head in understanding.

The journalist, however, did not acknowledge me. He was trying to get out of the bone-chilling water by sitting on the stern bench of his swamped canoe. This he managed to do for just a second. Then the canoe rolled and he fell back into the water.

Now his capsized canoe was between us, and as Rob grabbed onto our side gasping from the cold I could see that the journalist was going into hypothermic shock. I urged him to hold on, took the life preserver from underneath my seat and tried to toss it into his arms. My aim was slightly off and the preserver landed to his side. At that moment I could literally see the light go out of his eyes. He was no longer aware of what was happening, and could no sooner turn to grab the life preserver than fly to the moon. I had never seen a man die before, but I was seeing it now, and I was helpless to do anything about it. Then, as he began to sink beneath the lake's surface Roland's and Jeff's canoe sliced through the water to his side and Roland scooped his paddle under the journalist's arms. The man seized onto the paddle in a purely reflexive reaction, and a second later Jeff had him by the scruff of the neck.

The danger wasn't past. We had to get both men out of the water fast or they would die from temperature loss. Rob, a stout, rugged man, worked his way to our stern and started kicking, helping Nate and me as we paddled to shore. When we reached it we left Rob to stagger onto land, and went back to help

Roland and Jeff with the journalist. We got him to shore, too. Then we built a fire for them. They didn't stop shivering until that night.

A month later I was back in Costa Rica, where I hand-delivered a check for about four thousand dollars to the director of The Monteverde Conservation League. It wasn't nearly what I had hoped to raise, but I had learned my first lesson as a conservationist — money does not come easy. The League was happy to get the four thousand, though, and arranged for me to overnight in a cabin located at the head of a trail that passed through the fifty-thousand acre Penas Blancas forest. There I was to meet with the chief of park guards, Wolf Guinden, the next morning.

Wolf was an old-timer, a Quaker who had gone to prison in the fifties because he had refused to enter the draft. He had come to Costa Rica in the sixties, and remembered when the gravel road that wound up the west side of the mountain had been only a mule trail, and forest had clothed the slopes of Monteverde all the way down to the main highway. He admitted to me that he had chain-sawed down his fair share of trees over the years. But he had come to see the folly of his ways, and now took pains to do his part to protect what was left.

He led me into the heart of the Penas Blancas, setting a brisk pace. As we hiked he pointed out such things as tapir scat, a jaguar footprint, the hanging nests of oreopendula birds and a troop of spider monkeys. The terrain became more difficult as we progressed. The muddy trail took us up and down some very steep ridges, and we had to pick and choose our footholds carefully. Wolf was good at this, and it was only my long legs and natural athleticism that enabled me keep pace.

By midday we had reached the scenic overlook that was our goal. An expanse of forest spread as far as the eye could see. The crowns of hundred and seventy-five-foot trees emerged above the canopy like islands in a green ocean. There were jaguars prowling this wilderness. They stalked deer, peccary, tapir and armadillo. Cougar inhabited the Penas Blancas, too. Wolf told me farmers complained that the cats sometimes ranged into farmland and killed livestock. Also, told me, he had seen ten-foot boa constrictors in Penas Blancas, and marching columns of army ants that ate every critter in their path. They were accompanied by ant birds that ate whatever the ants scared up and couldn't catch, but never ate the ants themselves.

As we sat in our aerie and ate our lunch, I fiddled with a stick and Wolf said, "There's more to saving rainforests than just buying up places like Penas Blancas."

I asked what he meant, and he said that we needed to help local farmers keep their land productive so they wouldn't be tempted to squat in reserves and clear more forest for planting crops. Hungry people aren't going to respect park boundaries, he emphasized, and went on to say that was why The League had an agroforestry outreach program. The program helped farmers plant shelter belts, supplied them with new varieties of legumes — plants that enrich soil with nitrogen — and demonstrated polyculturing — intermixing several plant crops in the same field to reduce pest infestation.

The League had also established *viveros,* or tree nurseries. The trees from these viveros would be given to landowners to plant on their property. Some of the trees were fruit-bearing and would eventually provide food, some were hardwoods that would be grown for the timber harvest, and some were nitrogen-fixers that would be planted to reinvigorate used-up soil.

"It's amazing how fast some trees species grow in this climate," he concluded, "As much as ten feet a year."

We finished our lunch and packed up to go. On our way through a stand of bamboo I carelessly slapped my stick against a stalk, and a wood chip flew into my left eye before I could close it. I yelped and fell to my knees in pain and surprise. Wolf turned around to see what was wrong, and immediately came to my side. He took some cotton out of his backpack and told me to open my eye. I did and could see nothing but a filmy blur.

"How bad?" I asked.

As he dabbed the cotton in my eye, looking for splinters that might have pierced it, he said he didn't know, then added "I'm going to bandage it up."

After his administration of first aid we set off to find a doctor. Our progress was slow because the treacherous trail was very tricky for me to negotiate without the depth perception two eyes provided. I almost slipped down the muddy slopes several times, and Wolf said, "Be careful. I once had to carry one of my park guides out of here after he tripped and broke a leg. I wouldn't want to try it with a big guy like you."

It was growing dark by the time we were on level ground and closing in on the cabin. I stopped in the area where we had seen the jaguar track on the way in and asked Wolf, "Do you smell that?"

"What?"

"That odor, smells like something died."

"Can't smell a thing," Wolf rejoined.

"It's over this way." I led him off the trail and guided us toward the stink. They say people who lose their sight can hear better than the rest of us. Maybe they can smell better, too, because it seemed my olfactory senses were very acute this day.

"Okay," Wolf said. "I smell it now."

We came upon the carcass of a half-eaten peccary. "It's a jaguar's kill, and fresh," Wolf said. "Doesn't take long for a corpse to start rotting in this country." He looked into the gloom of the sur-rounding forest with knowing eyes. "She's probably in the neigh-borhood, we'd better move on."

I slept soundly in the cabin that night, exhausted from the long hike and resigned to the loss of my left eye. Fitting that the last thing I saw with it was a vista of unspoiled rainforest that was bursting with exuberant life.

Wolf got up early the next morning and fixed me a good breakfast. Then we started up the eastern slope of Monteverde. Along the we way joked about this and that, and I made light of my injury, telling him that as far as the ladies were concerned, the next best thing to a dueling scar on your cheek was a buccaneer's patch over an eye. But after we had returned to civilization and taken off the bandage I found that I could see again. I had only suffered an abrasion, and flew home to Wisconsin grateful that my stupidity had not cost me the use of an eyeball.

I learned the conservationist's second lesson during the next year: there's a lot of competition out there. I should have been happy about this, but wasn't. I felt the same territoriality that the Alaskan grad student had felt about his hawk owl research. The idea of uniting teachers and students to save rainforests was mine, and I pouted like a brat when I heard about Children's Rainforest – USA from the Monteverde League's director.

A biologist from a university in Maine, Sharon Kinsman conducted research in Monteverde. Sharon had founded her organization after a visit to Sweden in 1987, where she showed her slides to a classroom of children taught by Eha Kern. Sweden is one of the most progressive countries in the world, and when the children saw that rainforests were being wiped out they asked how they could help. Sharon told them they could raise money to buy Penas Blancas, so Eha Kern and her second graders started a grassroots campaign that swept the entire country. They raised over a million dollars and donated it to The Monteverde Conservation League. Sharon was trying to duplicate Eha's feat in the United States of America.

So, in part, was Cliff Ross, an elementary school teacher from New York City who founded The Earth's Birthday Project. I learned about Cliff through my association with the Wisconsin Chapter of The Nature Conservancy. Cliff wanted to unite children in a celebration of Earth Day every spring. The major component of his program was the raising and donating of money to The Nature Conservancy's "Adopt An Acre" program in Guatemala. Like Sharon and Eha, he was having much more success than I was.

No longer feeling like "the anointed one," I concentrated on registering teachers and high school students for the two week rainforest ecology courses I had set up with the Monteverde Institute for the following summer. I felt that the people from the schools that were sending us money should have a chance to see the forest they were helping to save. I also believed that when they returned to the United States of America they would share their experiences with others, which would help raise awareness about tropical forests and encourage people to donate more money for their preservation.

I wanted to show the pampered kids who came on the trips how good they had it back in the states, to make them realize how rich they were, how many unnecessary material possessions they had, and perhaps set them on the path of being environmentally conscious at home. It was hypocritical, I thought, to ask people in Third World countries to conserve their forests while we in the industrial nations were consuming 75 percent of the world's resources and polluting the earth's biosphere with our power plants, factories and automobiles.

I succeeding in filling each of the three scheduled courses with twenty people, and accompanied the first group to Monteverde. The course went extremely well. Students and teachers learned about plant life during walks in the forest. They had solo experiences where they were left alone on the trail to quietly soak in their surroundings. They transplanted trees from the vivero, and studied insects that were attracted to night-lights. They mist-netted bats under the expert supervision of a wonderful old character who told the students to be gentle when they untangled the bats from the net, warning them, "Be careful not to jerk your hand if they bite you, it might break their delicate teeth."

From Monteverde I flew to Belize to check out Programme for Belize (PFB), a newly founded conservation organization that was trying to buy up 110 thousand acres of rainforest in northwestern Belize before it was purchased and denuded of forest by the country's industrious Mennonite farmers or by citrus growers. I had heard about PFB from a science teacher in Colorado. I conferred with The Nature Conservancy's international division in Washington, D.C., which, along with the Massachusetts Audubon Society, had helped PFB get established, and set up a meeting with Joy Grant, PFB's director.

Joy and I talked about the 110 thousand-acre Rio Bravo region, and the importance of demonstrating that the forest could generate the income PFB would need to manage and protect it. "We would like to extract resin from *chicle* trees to produce "Rainforest Gum," Joy said, and in a buffer zone we would like to selectively harvest mahogany trees. We would do a forestry study first, to make sure we weren't doing any serious damage to the forest, then design a sustainable forestry plan that would allow us to harvest a modest number of trees each year. The income from mahogany would pay our bills and allow us to accomplish our main goal, the preservation of the Rio Bravo ecosystem."

I told Joy we would raise money to help them complete the land purchase at Rio Bravo. I also told her that we might be interested in having PFB conduct two-week ecology courses for us like the Monteverde Institute did in Costa Rica. This, I intimated, would provide PFB with the opportunity to earn eco-tourism, or more accurately, eco-education dollars on a yearly basis.

Joy was enthusiastic about my offer, and had her top man, John Masson, drive me out to Rio Bravo to have a look at their newly constructed station in the heart of the Rio Bravo Conservation Area. It served as a base of operations for the PFB field staff and visiting researchers.

John was a relic from the past, a talkative and charismatic vagabond who had done everything from managing Jamaican rum distilleries and sugar plantations to supervising the construction of Rio Bravo's rough gravel roads. He had originally come to Belize to hunt crocodiles and jaguars but, like Wolf Guinden, he had seen the error of his ways and had become a staunch conservationist.

John was a perfect guide, keeping me entertained with his stories, and speaking frankly about PFB and Rio Bravo. "It's a great outfit, all right, now dat dey got me to handle all de problems dat come up in de bush. But dis forest here ain't virgin. Don't go tinkin dat. It's been logged over fer Mahogany fer years. And dem Mennonites, dey ain't such bad sorts. Dey may clear off de forest but dey raise a good crop and I do a lotta business wid dem."

When we got to the station John showed me around the buildings and pointed out where PFB could construct a dormitory to house our students. Then we went for a walk on some nearby trails where John pointed out Strangler Figs, the scars that *chicleros* had made years ago on the trunks of chicle trees, and the mahogany trees that the loggers had missed. He said that the forest was in good shape, and bursting with wildlife. There were a lot of deer and peccary for the cougars and jaguars to eat, and a plentitude of fruit-bearing trees to feed the many parrots and toucans that called Rio Bravo home.

Following our walk he drove me up a side road to La Milpa, an unexcavated Mayan ruin where archaeologists were doing research. We walked around huge mounds of earth overgrown with vegetation. These mounds disguised the fabulous pyramids that had once marked the center of a great city. John explained that no one was sure why this city, why the entire Mayan civilization, had collapsed. Maybe it was due to the environmental problems associated with overpopulation. Estimates showed that three million Mayans had once inhabited what was now known as Belize, a country with a current population of only two hundred thousand.

"Dis is de court," he said, changing subjects, and indicating a field between two large mounds. "Dis is where dey played dere sacred ball game wid de ball made from chicle. De winner was rewarded by being sacrificed on de altar over dere."

After a good dinner of chicken and fried plantains, and an evening spent at the station over a bottle of John's best scotch, we headed back to Belize City. From there I caught a small twin engine aircraft that transported me to Dangriga, a small town down the coast. Then I was boated out to South Water Cay and left for two days with an ice chest of food, to see if this was a suitable site for my groups to spend the second half of their Belize course.

I decided pretty fast that it was. There was a nice sandy beach and plenty of shallow water where the participants of our course could learn to snorkel. There were also shallow reefs that exhibited the bright colors that the water absorbed as you dove deeper. And further out, the wall of Belize's barrier reef where you could free-dive down to barrel sponges that grew as big as a man, and see eagle rays cruise, pterodactyl-like, through a world of blue silence. On the island stood several buildings that served to house university groups during spring break, and would be adequate for our students during their summer visit.

I returned to Dodgeville excited about the new course I could offer to students and teachers in Belize. Then I drove a group of Wisconsin Academy of Science students to the Florida Keys for a ten-day coral reef field trip. I rented a duplex on Marathon Key, one side for the girls and one side for the boys, and an eighteen-foot boat. I spent a week teaching my Wisconsin high school students about echinoderms, coelenterates, crustaceans, marine annelids, plankton, mollusks, and fish. It was an unforgettable week for them, and for me, too. I was still encountering creatures I had never seen before. The primitive-looking horseshoe crab that Sarah, my top student on the trip, and I chased across a shallow sandy bottom was common, but for me a novel sight. The sea horse we happened to notice in some leafy sargassum weed was my first. And the eighteen-inch spotted nurse shark, which bit me when I pulled its tail to get it to move, was one of the two hundred and fifty or so species of shark that I hadn't previously come in contact with.

When our time was up I drove my students back to Wisconsin and bade them goodbye, but not before signing up Sarah for a trip to Costa Rica. Then I got to work on STR business. In addition to buying rainforest in Penas Blancas and Rio Bravo I wanted to offer our students a chance to help preserve forests through means other than simply purchasing land. I also wanted to expand our efforts to other parts of the world. I did some research and found two projects that were perfect for my purposes. One was a Rainforest Action Network project that supported an indigenous group in Sarawak, Malaysia called the Penan, in their struggle to defend their forest and their culture against a corrupt government that was granting illegal logging permits to Japanese logging companies on Penan lands. Another was World Wildlife Fund's anti-poaching program in the Central African Republic, where the Dzanga Sangha Reserve existed on paper but was subject to incursions by hunters who would shoot chimpanzees and gorillas for meat and novelty items like gorilla-hand ashtrays, and kill forest elephants for their ivory.

I added descriptions of these new conservation programs to the teacher's guide I was now sending out to over ten thousand schools, and returned a call from Larry Rockefeller, one of *the* Rockefellers. His environmental organization, the American Conservation Association, was sponsoring something called Children's Earth Fund (CEF). CEF wanted to unite under one umbrella the children's environmental groups that were suddenly proliferating like rabbits. By so doing we could, among other things, gather a lot of signatures on a petition asking George Bush to attend the upcoming Earth Summit in Rio de Janeiro. We could also circulate a pledge card on which individuals would indicate how they planned to reduce the carbon dioxide emissions they were personally responsible for creating.

This uniting of forces was not a bad idea. There were now at least a half-dozen organizations vying for the attention of school children, sometimes working at cross purposes, sometimes duplicating efforts. A partial list: Save The Rainforest, Inc., Children's Rainforest-USA, Earth's Birthday Project, C.A.P.E., Kids Face, and Clinton Hill's Kids for Saving Earth.

After a long telephone conversation with Larry I agreed to circulate his petition and come to Washington, D.C. the following summer to join with the other groups in presenting our signatures in person to the President of the United States.

Not long after this, school started up again. I was so busy with STR that I barely had time to teach, and by the second semester it became apparent that I couldn't serve two masters. The prospect of quitting the classroom didn't bother me, but I wondered if STR could come close to matching the salary the school paid. I was insistent that every penny school children sent us go directly to projects earmarked by their school. That left the margin we made on the courses and whatever grants we got our only income for covering operational expenses and a salary for me. Would it be enough for me to live on?

With this question on my mind I flew to Washington where I met Larry and the leaders of the other organizations listed previously. Larry was a thoughtful host, and organized our activities with great care. He didn't get us in to see President Bush but he was able to arrange a meeting with Senator Al Gore. What impressed me the most about Larry was his picking up the garbage that spilled out of a trash can in the reception room where Al Gore met us. It was the garbage our delegation had overstuffed the container with as we ate lunch, and he felt responsible for it. This, I thought, said a lot for a man who was a multimillionaire and already had his hands full with running our show.

All the leaders of the groups were interesting. I had met Cliff Ross on a prior occasion at the suggestion of The Nature Conservancy, an organization we were both donating funds to now. Cliff was a really decent, soft-spoken person who was as committed as I was to educating young people and giving them the opportunity to take action to save rainforests. We had come to the conclusion that although our efforts sometimes overlapped, we were compatible with each other, and we had decided to support the Rio Bravo land purchase in Belize together.

I had never before met the three women who directed the other groups. I liked two of them. The third, Mrs. Hill, I didn't. She was a bit too overbearing in her attempt to dominate our little cartel. Her group, Clinton Hill's Kids for Saving Earth, had been founded in honor of her son, who had died of cancer. Before Clinton died he had been the driving force behind a school environmental club. In a classic case of serendipity Mrs. Hill had approached Target Department Stores at just the right time with the idea that they should sponsor a kids' environmental club. Target handed her a check for a million dollars. I think this windfall convinced Mrs. Hill that her son's death had been for a high purpose, and that Clinton Hill's Kids for Saving Earth would single-handedly save the earth. As a result she looked upon the rest of us as disciples. She even offered Cliff and me jobs if we would subjugate ourselves to her. Cliff and I both turned her down, and accurately predicted that she would fritter away her million dollars on expensive color brochures with Clinton's name plastered all over them. It was a little pathetic and frustrating, too, because Cliff and I were struggling along on shoestring budgets and could have done a lot with a million dollars. But this was my third conservationist lesson: money *can* come easy.

At the end of our summit I took Larry aside and asked him for seventy-five hundred dollars to set up STR's office in my home. He said he would have his American Conservation Association cut me a check, and with his promise of support I called up Dodgeville High School and resigned. Then I got on a plane to fly to Ecuador and investigated an organization called Fundacion Jatun Sacha (FJS), which had been co-founded by Mike McColm. Mike had telephoned me after seeing an article in *Parade Magazine*. The article focused on Eha Kern's having won a Goldman Environmental Award for her work in Sweden, but also mentioned me. He wanted STR to support land purchase at their site in the upper Amazon, and to conduct courses at their station. I agreed to give their site a look over, and was glad I did.

One of the other co-founders of Fundacion Jatun Sacha was Dr. David Neil, a brilliant botanist that was a senior fellow with Missouri Botanical Gardens. He met me at the airport in Quito, Ecuador. The next day we drove into the Andes, through a thirteen thousand-foot pass and down into the Amazonian basin to the FJS field station, located along the Rio Napo, a major tributary of the Amazon River.

David hadn't really wanted to get caught up in the politics, fund raising and administration that came with running a foundation, but he, Mike and Alejandro, the third co-founder, just couldn't stand by and let a treasure like Jatun Sacha, the Quichua term for "great forest," be destroyed. The three of them emptied

their pockets to buy a few hundred hectares of the forest, built a
rude field station, incorporated as an Ecuadorian nonprofit foundation and began to solicit donations so they could purchase more
hectares.

When I saw the place I fell in love with it. This was one of the
very few places on earth where you could encounter *two hundred
and fifty species* of trees in a single hectare. One of those species
was the giant kapok tree that rose out of the earth obelisk like to
a height of two hundred feet, and had a circumference of some
thirty feet at its base. There were, according to a herpetologist
doing an inventory there, sixty-seven species of frogs here. The
racket they caused at night attested to his veracity. An ornitholo-
gist had catalogued four hundred and eighty species of birds, and
a mycologist two thousand species of fungi. This place was the
mother lode of diversity, Dr. Neil told me, and I could believe it.
Everywhere I looked there were different species of butterflies
fluttering about, different kinds of grasshoppers jumping from
leaf to leaf. Alejandro showed me his collection of orchids; there
were countless species of them, too.

"We'll help," I said after my first day, and Alejandro put his
finger to his lips.

He told me that buying the land for a good price was a tricky
business, and if the locals found out there was a lot of money
floating around, the cost of a hectare would skyrocket. It would
be better if no one along the Napo River knew that STR was
donating money to FJS for land purchase. I nodded my head
conspiratorially, pleased to be in cahoots with the Alejandro. If
FJS didn't buy the land it would be deforested by tenants who
could get a cattle subsidy for clearing their property, even if they
never raised any cattle on it, which most of them didn't because it
wasn't profitable. The highway robbery we were committing by
paying only the going rate of seventy dollars per acre for some of
the richest habitat on the planet, was pretty innocent compared
to cutting down the forest for a subsidy. And the tenants wouldn't
have sold us the land at all if they could have benefited more by
doing something else with it.

Next we talked about the possibility of STR bringing students to the site. Both Alejandro and David liked the idea because
they thought Jatun Sacha was a very special place, and they wanted

people to see it. They also knew that our courses would generate funds for them every summer, and enable the foundation to employ local people. I added that most of our participants brought extra money that they spent in the community. In addition we asked students to bring educational supplies to donate to the poor rural schools in the area. Alejandro really liked this; he had two children himself, and he knew that simple things, like paper, crayons, rulers, pens and scissors, were highly prized in Napo Province.

"You know what?" Alejandro then said. "We should include an overnight visit to a Quichua village in your courses. Capirona would be the perfect place."

"That sounds really interesting," I said. "Where's Capirona?"

"That way," he said, pointing southeast.

David added, "The only way to get there is to walk, and that would take three to four hours, or take a canoe down the Napo till you get to the Rio Arajuno, then paddle upriver to the village."

"The village could demonstrate the use of blowguns, their face-painting traditions, and dances," Alejandro brainstormed.

"I don't want it to turn into a show for tourists," I said.

Alejandro replied, "Nor me. I think we should have your groups spend some time helping the Quichua in their garden plots. That would be a real learning experience for them. And you should tell your students to be prepared to share something of their own culture with the Quichua — a song, a story, something like that."

"I think that would be great," I said.

"We'll have to pay a visit to the village and talk to the elders about it," David interjected.

"Okay, how about tomorrow?" I asked.

The next morning it was raining hard, as it often did at Jatun Sacha. We waited till it let up a bit, then David and I set off on the trail to Capirona. David was tall and lanky, and walked the trail with long, easy strides. The trail was one of many that crisscrossed the forest, and as we followed it we left our world behind. There was nothing in the direction we were going but the seemingly endless Amazon forest, and a few scattered native villages. It was true that much of the Amazon had been cut down, and that it was continuing to be depleted, but we had left the frontier of destruction to our rear. Ahead of us were five hundred miles of wilderness, inhabited by Quichua, and further out, by the warlike Huaorani, hunter-gatherers who had only recently stopped killing outsiders.

We came to a fork in the trail. David stopped, rubbed his chin, and said rather uncertainly, "I think it's this way."

As we continued on it started raining very hard again. Over the sound of the rain David talked about what interested him most, trees. He told me that the high diversity of tree life here meant that the population density of a particular species was usually quite low. This posed a problem for the trees when it came time to reproduce, because often the nearest member of their species was a mile or more distant. The forest didn't allow for pollination by wind, and it was highly unlikely that a pollinating insect, hummingbird or bat would end up visiting two trees that were so far apart — unless they had to. But over millions of years of evolution many pollinators had become dependent on a particular tree's flower, and would fly straight from one tree to another of the same species even if it meant covering great distances.

"Imagine how complex it's all become," he finished. "How marvelous. Look at all these trees, all these ground plants, vines, lianas and epiphytes. We don't know how many of them are associated with insect "specialists," and we may never know. But that illustrates how intricate the ecology of the rainforest is, and how fragile."

We came to a stream that was running high. We stopped on its bank, and David rubbed his chin again. "Hmph," he exclaimed. "I've only been to Capirona once."

Thinking we might have to turn back, I tried to remember the way we had come, but the trails seemed like a maze to me, and apparently to David. I had visions of wandering deep into the Amazon until we eventually trespassed on Huaorani territory, and were speared for our troubles.

"We'll cross here I guess," David said.

This statement did not inspire very much confidence, but I held his pack for him, and he started to wade across. The water was deeper and the current stronger than he anticipated, and it swept him off his feet. He had to swim to make it to the other side. I was getting ready to throw him both our packs and swim across myself when I heard a voice behind me. I swiveled my head and saw a smiling, barefoot boy in shorts and a ragged T-shirt, holding a rusty shotgun that was as tall as he.

It turned out that Capirona had heard that David and I were coming for a visit and had sent this youngster to meet and escort us to them. A good thing, too, because we were way off course by the time he tracked us down. With him as our guide we retraced our steps, got on the right series of trails and arrived in Capirona by mid-afternoon. The boy's father, who spoke Spanish, in which David was fluent, greeted us and invited us to sit down. As David talked with him about our course, the man nodded, then indicated to his wife to bring a bowl of fermented manioc for us to drink. The woman dipped a ladle into a caldron of thick, white fluid and filled a bowl. It was passed around much as American plains Indians had passed around peace pipes a century and a half ago. After my first sip I noticed the woman spitting into the caldron and stirring her saliva into the manioc beer. This was intended to sweeten it.

After we emptied the bowl, another was filled, then another. Finally David put an end to this hospitality by asking if it wasn't time to meet the elders. The man, a little inebriated, said that it was indeed. He sent his son to summon the elders to the community lodge, and led us there to rendezvous with them. When everyone had assembled the speech-making began. First, our interpreter introduced David, who gave a short explanation of what we were proposing. Our friend translated this. The elders listened gravely, looked at me, and said a few things among themselves. Then one of the elders got up and gave a talk that lasted 20 minutes. The gist of it was that the village of Capirona would be pleased and honored to receive my young people as guests.

At this juncture a second elder presented me with a flask of homemade liquor. I took a drink suppressed a grimace, and returned it. Then the elder proffered the poison to David, who followed my example, after which all the elders took a drink. I was called on to give a speech next. I kept it short because it was getting late, and David and I had to get started back to the station in time to beat the dark. We were delayed another fifteen minutes, however, by another speech that formally recapped our agreement. It was five o'clock before we were allowed to depart.

The little boy guided us almost all the way back to the station. When he was absolutely certain we were on a trail we could not possibly stray from, he bid us adieu and headed back to Capirona in the gathering dusk. A half-hour later we traipsed into camp, tired and hung over. We went to the mess hall to get some grub, and found that a birthday party for the herpetologist was in progress. As we congratulated him I was reminded of the day's date; it was June 20th, and my birthday, too. I had almost passed my thirty-sixth birthday without taking notice of it.

Tom Wohl drinking from Liana in Dzanga
Sangha Reserve in the Central African Republic

CHAPTER TWENTY-FOUR

SALT OF THE EARTH

Rainforests absorb great amounts of carbon dioxide
from the atmosphere and can help reduce global warming.
However, when rainforests are cut down and burned they
actually add carbon dioxide to the atmosphere.
— Save the Rainforest fact sheet

In my thirty-seventh summer I traveled to Monteverde again, to participate in a conference hosted by he Monteverde Conservation League. Other participants included Eha and Bernd Kern, from the Swedish group Barnens Regnskog, Robin and Tina Jollife, from Children's Rainforest, UK, Sharon Kinsman, from Children's Rainforest – USA, Daniel Hub, from Kinderregnwal Duetschland, and Mineohara-Kogen Suzaka, from Nippon Kodomo No Jungle. Dave Younkman, from the Latin American Division of The Nature Conservancy, was also in attendance, but only as an observer.

All the participating organizations except STR were offshoots of Barnends Regnskog, and Bernd Kern, its director, played the main role at our conference. He didn't like or trust me because STR had sprung up independently of him, and because a Swedish organization called Save The Rainforest had done harm to Barnends Regnskog and it's cause. They copied Bernd's fundraising techniques and then caused a scandal by keeping most of the money they raised to pay their officers exorbitant salaries. This incident illustrates the conservationist's fourth lesson: Success is imitated, and sometimes the imitator is unscrupulous.

Bernd didn't like David Younkman from The Nature Conservancy very much either. TNC was a big, sophisticated organization run in an efficient and professional manner. This kind of organization rubbed Bernd the wrong way. He was unrealistically hard on any environmental organization that he thought was allocating money for offices, secretaries, marketing, scientific research, program analysis, and salaries instead of for land purchase and direct program support.

At the behest of Robin and Tina, who had become my good friends, Bernd grudgingly allowed STR into the association we formed at a conference called International Children's Rainforest Network (ICRN). We agreed on some common guidelines for supporting conservation projects that TNC's David Younkman helped us draft. Here are some of the guidelines: Projects must protect forests of high quality and diversity; projects must protect highly endangered and rare forests; projects must be overseen by an effective conservation partner; projects must have good prospects for long-term success; and projects must be in relatively stable countries so they can't be undermined by politics.

We also promised to support one another's projects whenever possible. I made good on that promise by supporting Children's Rainforest, UK's reforestation program in Thailand; UK, Sweden and Germany eventually provided crucial monies to my friends at Fundacion Jatun Sacha (FJS).

Not long after this conference I received an unsolicited letter from the Joan Irvine Smith And Athlaie R. Clarke Foundation, asking me what STR would do with a hundred thousand dollars. I replied that I would invest eighty thousand in building or improving stations in the rainforest. The other twenty thousand would help with our operational expenses over the next two years. Two weeks after replying I had in my hand a hundred thousand dollar check from the foundation. About half of that money went to FJS in Ecuador and PFB in Belize. I donated the rest to ANCON, a conservation organization in Panama, so they could build a rainforest station near Sobernia National Park, in the Canal Zone, where ANCON would host some of our future groups.

Things were rolling along pretty well now. We had fifteen thousand schools on our mailing list, we were members of the ICRN, we were sending seven hundred and fifty students and teachers on our courses each summer, and school children were sending us over a hundred thousand dollars every year for conservation projects. Then Curt Clemenson came along. In Houston, Texas, he had formed a group called Earth Foundation that was a local chapter of the Rainforest Action Network. He decided to expand into a nationwide organization, and raise funds in schools for the rainforest.

I didn't find out about his "Race to the Rescue" campaign until I got a call from Cliff Ross saying we had better watch out for Earth Foundation. I told Cliff not to worry, but that was a mistake. A year later Earth Foundation was raising three times as much money for land purchase as STR was, and touting itself as the organization leading a crusade to save rainforests. Earth Foundation was also offering student adventure tours to the rainforest, and to my dismay I learned that one of their groups was scheduled to visit our station in Panama during a time period I had reserved for STR. I called ANCON; they apologized and rescheduled Curt's group. But now I knew I had some competition.

Cliff Ross, of Earth's Birthday Project, knew he had some competition, too. By the time another year had passed, Curt was raising a million dollars a year-twice what Cliff raised-and was pressuring The Nature Conservancy to give Earth Foundation an exclusive contract to represent their "Adopt an Acre" program in schools. This was a program with which Cliff was symbiotically involved, a program to which he had donated a couple of million dollars, and a program he couldn't do without.

While all this was going on I learned that a commercial tour operator in Belize, International Zoological Expeditions, had all but plagiarized our ecology course program, and had been promoted in the literature of Project Jason, Robert Ballard's educational exploration series that showed in schools all over the United States. I made an angry phone call and asked the staff if they knew or cared that their profiling of a commercial tour operator was undermining our work to save rainforest in Belize. They pleaded to the lesser charge of ignorance, and I told them that in the future they had better do more research before collaborating with questionable outfits like IZE.

"For God's sake," I chastised them one last time before hanging up, "your series on Belize completely missed the most important thing going on there, Programme for Belize's innovative management of a quarter-million acres (PFB had acquired an additional hundred and forty thousand acres) of critical rainforest habitat. If Robert Ballard had operated like you guys do he would have never discovered the Titanic.

Joy Grant, director of PFB, was pretty upset about the Project Jason incident, too. She told me the damage was done, though. She then added that one of my board members had recently approached her with an offer to supplant the STR courses with those he planned to organize through a foundation he'd newly set up. He had visited her in her office after completing a Save The Rainforest course, said he could do a better job for PFB than STR, and that his foundation would donate a hundred thousand dollars to PFB if they would make the switchover. Joy had declined his generosity because she didn't want to work with a person like that, but she thought I should know about the matter. I thanked her.

That board member's infidelity was shocking, but it hadn't hurt STR like Earth Foundation and IZE. In the next year our course registrations dropped to five hundred and fifty and our fundraising dipped below the seventy-five thousand dollar level. I decided to get more assertive, and began to employ some of Curt's tactics, renting booths at teachers' conventions, where I displayed banners about how great we were, selling T-shirts and making rainforest videos to send out to schools. I was careful not to make disparaging remarks about Earth Foundation, though, because I didn't want to start a war, and distract people from the real issue at hand, rainforest destruction. Eventually Curt turned Earth Foundation into a for-profit business and sold it for a substantial sum.

Around this time I met Kim, whose sister Lisa was married to my friend Kevin. Lisa arranged for the four of us to go out to a country-western joint one Saturday night. We danced all evening, and on the way home Kim and I expressed our newfound affection for one another in the back seat.

Kim was cute and perky. She lived with her three children in a small mobile home in the hillbilly country just south of La Crosse. Her oldest child was the daughter of a man she had fallen in love with while she was very young. Tyler, her hyperactive seven-year old, and Kaylani, her darling six-year old, were the children of another man, whom she had recently divorced.

On our second date she told me she had been ready to give up on men before meeting me. On our third date I think she fell in love with me. After that she started driving the sixty miles from La Crosse to Dodgeville every other weekend to see me. These were the weekends her ex-husband had Tyler and Kaylani. We were complete opposites and I don't know why we got along so well, maybe it was just physical. But I think there was more to it than that. I think that we cared about each other. Each of us had a good sense of humor, too, and we laughed a lot about our differences.

That summer I left Kim for ten days to travel to Sweden to attend our second ICRN conference. I joined Daniel, Robin and Mineohara on the Kern's Storybook Farmette, just south of Stockholm. There we reviewed what we had done for the last two years, and planned what to do in the future. This was the conference where it was decided Jatun Sacha would be our next major joint project. Between business sessions Robin and Bernd did an enormous amount of smoking, eating and drinking.

"They work hard," I thought, "and they play hard."

But for Robin the drinking was also a way to temporarily forget about the loss of his wife, Tina, to cancer. It was she who had founded Children's Rainforest, UK, and he was keeping it going out of respect for her memory. At any rate, while Robin and Bernd emptied bottle after bottle of wine, Mineohara and Eha cooked, and Daniel and I bicycled through the scenic countryside and swam in the cold lakes. Daniel and I also took the train into Stockholm where I bought some gifts to take back to Kim.

Kim was thrilled with her presents, and happy to have me back in her arms. She came down to Dodgeville every weekend now, bringing Tyler and Kaylani along when they weren't with their dad. Kim's oldest daughter had moved in with her biological father and his new wife.

I developed a real fondness for Kim's children. Tyler was a little imp with a predilection for getting in trouble. He got caught shoplifting, was constantly in hot water at school for not doing his homework, and had once playfully thrown a stick at his mother, which hit her in the eye, requiring treatment at the hospital emergency room. Still, I couldn't help feeling a fatherly affection for him. Loving Kaylani was no challenge at all. She was a stereotypical, sweet six-year old girl, who liked lollipops, pink dresses, horsy-back rides, being read to and getting tucked in at night. After a year of being their part-time daddy I told Kim I wanted her and the kids to move in with Cassandra and me.

She had to get approval from the children's court-appointed guardian to move them so far away from their real dad, but she got it, and now I had a family on my hands. It was quite an adjustment for an old bachelor like me to suddenly have a house full of people living with me on a day-in, day-out basis. But I gradually adapted to the chaos around me and began to like it. So did Cassandra. She never tired of chasing after the balls Kaylani and Tyler tossed around the backyard, and she was always in the lead when I took "my family" for a walk to the creek to watch red-winged blackbirds balancing on cattails, and to examine the exposed mud banks for raccoon, skunk and opossum tracks.

Cassandra would accompany Tyler and me to Governor Dodge, too. We'd pile into the car, drive out to the park where I knew of a trail leading to one of the lakes, and unload Tyler's bicycle, which he then pedaled to the lake while Cassandra and I ran. When the three of us got to the lake we split up: I went for a long swim, Cassandra investigated the shoreline with her nose, and Tyler fished. This was his favorite thing in the whole world to do, and he told me he wanted someday to catch a big northern like the one I had hanging on my wall.

These excursions tailed off when the school year started. Tyler and Kaylani attended Dodgeville Elementary and Kim began classes in nursing at Fennimore Technical School. She had to get up and drive away in her Corsica every morning at 6:00 A.M., and it was left to me to rouse "our" children, see that they got dressed, feed them, fix them a sack lunch and send them out the door in time to catch the bus. This could be quite a three-ring circus. Kaylani was very fussy about her appearance, and I would often find her standing in front of the bathroom mirror with a frown on her face when she should have been kissing me on the cheek at the door and saying goodbye.

Tyler would usually refuse to get up until I detonated an atomic bomb under his butt. Then he'd be unable to find his other sock, or his geography book, or remember where his backpack was. Somehow I would always find the elusive object, and get him on his way, a shoelace untied perhaps, to school with Kaylani.

This routine, of course, was interrupted every weekend. On alternate weekends Kaylani and Tyler's dad picked them up. On those weekends Kim and I would sometimes drive into Madison to dine at an intimate little place called Casa de Lara, where we were always serenaded by the guitarist. If we didn't go out we'd have a candlelit dinner at home, replete with bottle of good wine, and romantic music.

This didn't last, though. We were just too different to make it work. Kim liked the TV on, I liked it off. She believed in God and the teachings of Pastor Murry on channel X, I didn't. She was lax with the children, I wanted them to do their homework and go to bed on time: She was messy, I was fastidious. I liked to recycle, she didn't. I bought the children erector sets and spelling games for Christmas, she bought them plastic space guns and beeping maze hand-computers: I read Proust, she read tabloids. She wanted to get married right away, I wanted more time to think about it.

On January 7, 1995 we called it quits. Kim didn't move out of the house because it would have looked very bad to the children's court guardian, and she was afraid of losing custody of them to her ex. So we began a strange coexistence, acting normal around the kids but sleeping apart, and going our separate ways on weekends.

In March I left her for a week to drive the passenger van STR was donating to Fundacion Prolansate down to Honduras. Roland, whom I had cultivated as a close friend, helped me drive the vehicle to its destination. I had taken pains to know Roland better because, among other things, he had played the part of Matthew in *Sinister Minister?* so realistically. Roland seemed to be the living embodiment of my better half; he considered the consequences of his actions with a sense of rectitude that was sometimes intimidating. He didn't want to have any children because the world was already too overpopulated. He kept his frugally furnished apartment at sixty degrees in winter because he thought it was sinful to waste energy. He worked as a successful stonemason, but refused to hire helpers because he didn't want to make money off the labor of others. Roland bore a striking resemblance to Robert Redford, but wouldn't lie to the women who were attracted to him about the likelihood of a long-term relationship that would end in marriage.

When Roland and I returned to Wisconsin, Kim was engaged to a twenty-seven year old boy she had met at a Halloween party the previous fall and kept in storage until he was needed. Her ex-husband heard about this and petitioned the guardian for custody of Tyler and Kaylani, basing his claim on the fact that Kim was living with one man and engaged to another. A court appearance was scheduled for June, whereupon I asked Kim to reconsider her betrothal and try one more time to make a go of it with me so she wouldn't lose her kids. She sat on my lap while I proposed this, as she had many times in the past when bad grades or some other thing had upset her and she needed comfort. But with tears in her eyes she said no; she had promised Matt she would marry him, and fight her lousy ex-husband and his petition. She'd convince the court that she was a good mother and that she and Matt would provide a good home for Kaylani and Tyler.

Then she said, "You'll testify that I'm a good mother won't you?"

"Of course I will," I assured her, and I did. But my testimony was deemed superfluous, and the judge awarded custody to Kim's ex. On the courthouse steps Kim, in her pretty flower-print dress, wept unrestrainedly as Matt, two of her sisters and I looked on helplessly.

"I can't believe they took my babies away," she uttered pitifully. Two weeks later she dumped Matt for a twenty-year old part-time construction worker who, I think, served both as a lover and as a child she could care for.

I was left to my own devices again, and filled my spare hours with swimming, biking, exercising to the aerobic tapes Kim had turned me on to, and teaching myself to sketch. I added piano lessons to that list of activities a little later, and fancied that I might yet find love, perhaps while playing Beethoven's *Moonlight Sonata* to a romantic young lady.

I took a vacation from piano lessons that winter to travel to

the Central African Republic to make a video about the Dzanga
Sangha Reserve. I planned to distribute it to the schools that had
supported World Wildlife Fund's anti-poaching program there.
Tom Wohl, the son of a friend and a former captain of the Notre
Dame swim team, volunteered to come along and help me at his
own expense. We flew to Bengui, the C.A.R.'s capital, via Paris,
where we made a two-day stopover to adjust our biorhythms,
sample French pastry and visit Notre Dame Cathedral, the Lou-
vre, and the Moulin Rouge.

Bengui was more a vast, impoverished native village than the
capital of a nation-state. Only a couple of hotels, a few restaurants
and businesses and half a dozen government buildings had elec-
tricity and plumbing. The rest of the city relied on kerosene lan-
terns, outdoor latrines, and wells dug in front yards. *Petro* was sold
in lemonade-like roadside stands in old wine bottles, goats were
herded along the mostly unpaved and dusty streets, and legless
beggars slid around on tattered squares of cardboard.

Tom and I spent the night in the World Wildlife Fund's office/
guest room in Bengui. Then we set out on the all-day journey to
Dzanga Sangha in a rugged land rover with our driver and a
Peace Corps worker who hitched a ride with us — there was no
bus service where we were going. As we drove along, the Peace
Corps worker told us about her country: median annual income
was twelve hundred dollars; average life span was forty-seven years;
the school system had been shut down for three years; and the
self-styled emperor of the Central African Republic had just fled
the country. C.A.R., she went on, was one of the most backward
countries in Africa, and where we were going, well, that was sort
of the end of the world. Just south of the Dzanga Sangha was a
swampy wilderness that even the pygmies, or BaAka, as she more
accurately referred to them, had not ventured into.

We almost got stuck in a sandy part of the so-called road that
turned off a so-called main highway to Dzanga Sangha. After
that we left the savanna behind us, a savanna empty of the hundred thousand white rhinos that had once inhabited it, and entered into a transitional zone between sparsely wooded grassland
and the dense forests of Africa's Congo Basin. By nightfall we
arrived at World Wildlife Fund's Dzanga Sangha station and were
greeted by Allard Bloom, the head honcho there. Allard put us up

in his office/living quarters in a room with bunk beds that also served as a place for storing supplies. In the morning his cook prepared us breakfast, complete with a glass of juice that had been slightly chilled in a decrepit gas-powered refrigerator which, while incapable of truly refrigerating, was a wonder to all the Bantu villagers in the neighborhood who were allowed a look at it.

Allard supplied us with a guide and the keys to the Land Rover, and told us the best place to begin our filming was the Dzanga Saline. This was a football-field-sized clearing that forest elephants had created as they excavated and ate the soil, which contained the salt and other minerals their bodies need. I drove the rover down an old logging road to within a half-mile of the saline, and we walked in the rest of the way. We came upon a colony of termites that I stopped to film with my macro lens. I wanted our video to show children the forest's smallest creatures as well as the biggest, and to inform them of the vital role of termites — and the bacteria in their guts — in breaking down the cellulose in wood and recycling dead trees.

We continued on toward the saline, the guide leading, Tom, carrying my tripod, bringing up the rear. We reached the saline shortly after wading through a wetland that was conveniently crocodile-less. Before we caught our first glimpse of the elephants we smelled them. A hundred elephants defecating in one area day after day leave their odorous mark. The elephant dung also leaves a legacy, for the elephants eat many seeds that end up sprouting out of their offal. This was one reason biologists called these forest elephants a keystone species. Like my beavers back in Wisconsin, they were the architects of their world. Not only did the elephants establish salines and distribute seeds, but they also created a network of wide trails through the forest. They tore down trees here and there as they fed, opening up areas where nutritious secondary vegetation could grow and feed animals like the giant forest hog, water buffalo and lowland gorilla.

I filmed the sixty or so elephants milling around the saline for about two hours. Intermixed with the elephants were a few forest antelope and a water buffalo that had come to the clearing to lap up some salt as well. The next day I came early to film the African Gray Parrots that arrived with the dawn in huge flocks, filling the saline's arena with a reverberating din, and pecking at the ground for their salt fix.

On day three our Bantu guide hired two BaAka trackers, and we drove to a remote research site at the end of a logging road where gorillas and chimpanzees were likely to be found. We reached this site at dusk, and before settling into a couple of thatch huts went down the hill to look over a small saline that was empty at the moment. We walked into the middle of the saline. I felt a little naked in the open, and kept looking around for a bad-tempered bull elephant to emerge from the forest and chase us out of his domain. At the edge of the saline our BaAka guides pointed out gorilla tracks. The next day promised good filming, and we retired to our huts, which had been investigated, pushed against and tilted askew by the curious elephants that had visited the camp over the years when it was uninhabited by researchers. I slept well in our hut, waking up once to the dinosaur-like trumpeting of elephants in the saline down the hill from us, and thinking how primordial this place was.

The gorilla that had left its prints didn't come back in the morning, and our BaAka trackers led us off into the forest to find us something to film. We walked for hours in this direction and that, and certainly would have been hopelessly lost had our trackers decided to abandon us. But they had no intention of doing that. They were good-natured, friendly men who seemed to enjoy sharing their jungle secrets with us, and it was with much excitement that they indicated to us a solitary female gorilla with her infant high in a tree above us. Tom set up the tripod, and I mounted the video camera on it and started rolling tape. The female shifted her position as soon as I had focused on her, and we had a lot of work to do before we finally got the footage I wanted. Then I let our trackers peek through the telephoto lens. They laughed with delight at the magnified view of their fellow forest creature. We all returned to camp in a good mood that night, and feasted on manioc paste, saltine crackers and a mixture of macaroni and canned tomatoes, which Tom and I scooped up with the lids of Pringles potato chip containers and which our native allies ate with their bare fingers.

Next day we set forth in search of a chimpanzee troop. We weren't having much luck so the trackers sat us down and tried calling in some chimps by imitating the birthing sounds of the duiker, a small species of antelope whose newborn calves the chimps would eat when they could. The calls attracted only another nervous duiker. Toward the end of the day the trackers cocked their ears to hear a sound that Tom and I couldn't make out. They motioned for us to hurry along after them, and in half an hour we were approaching a troop of chimpanzees feeding in the treetops high above us.

As I mounted the camera to start shooting, the chimps ceased feeding and concealed themselves from view. They made vocalizations that the BaAka responded to. This seemed to upset the chimps — precisely the reaction the BaAka wanted, for the agitated troop began to scold us in high-pitched shrieks and expose themselves as they threw bits of debris and excrement at us. I missed most of this action but was able capture the amazingly rapid descent of a couple of individuals from treetop to forest floor. Then I got a great shot of the dominant male as he walked out onto a large limb just above me. A second later he vanished behind some branches, and then crashed to the forest floor where he took flight with the rest of his comrades.

When we returned to the Dzanga Sangha station, Allard was surprised and pleased that we'd gotten footage of both chimpanzees and gorillas. He was just as eager to show off the wildlife of Dzanga Sangha to school children as we were, and to explain that, without the presence of the rangers hired by WWF, poachers would infiltrate the reserve and kill all the animals, especially those that frequented the exposed salines.

After breakfast the next morning Tom and I went for a stroll down the gravel road that had brought us to Dzanga Sanhga. We came upon a column of driver ants crossing the road. There were millions of them. Some interlocked their legs to form a tunnel that the main body streamed through to the other side of the road. Others skirmished three feet to either side of the tunnel, viciously attacking anything they encountered. Allard had told us these ants would clean a tethered goat down to the bone in one hour. Tom and I ran back to the office to get the camera and tripod. When we returned twenty minutes later the driver ants were still crossing the road. Their numbers seemed endless, and as I filmed the main column its skirmishers assaulted me. I did what

Tom called an "ant dance," hopping from one foot to the other in an effort to keep the ants from crawling up my legs. This didn't do much good, and I soon retreated from the scene, leaving the camera running to film whatever it filmed, and requesting that Tom brush the ants off me. Some of their bites had drawn blood.

Allard suggested we next travel down the Sangha River to WWF's most isolated outpost at the southernmost tip of the reserve. He arranged to have us transported down river with our guide and two trusty trackers. It was during this journey that Tom began complaining about dizzy spells and lightheadedness. He thought it might be malaria. I said that if it was we needed to get him some medical attention right away. But he shook his head, saying it was probably nothing.

We got to the outpost late in the afternoon, and briefly reconnoitered the area around camp. Then the outpost manager's wife, whom we had picked up en route on the Cameroon side of the river, cooked dinner for us. Afterward we sat in the dusk on the riverbanks as our guide fished, big fruit bats flew overhead and gorillas roared goodnight to the world from the fastness of the forest on the other side of the river. We retired soon after the roaring subsided, but didn't get much sleep because there was a cricket in our hut that emitted a loud monotonous trill that sounded like the irritating emergency signal broadcast as a public service on radio stations. Every time I got up to search it out with my flashlight it ceased its trilling, having evolved over the eons, I ruefully concluded, to keep quiet when being stalked by angry, sleepless filmmakers with murder in their hearts.

Tom felt worse in the morning, but attributed it to a bad night's sleep, and we spent the day trekking through the hot forest, sweating like pigs, and not seeing any wildlife worth filming. The BaAka trackers found a pair of tortoises they were interested in, though. They let the female go on her way to lay the eggs they said she carried. The male they trussed up with a vine and carried back to the outpost. They made a feast of the reptile, and the store-bought saltine crackers and canned tomatoes we gave them. Afterward they sat against a tree trunk and contentedly smoked a couple of the cigarettes we'd given them. This was as good as it got for a BaAka. Tom and I had some macaroni and finished off our last container of precious Pringles.

I slept soundly that night, for my cricket friend had either vacated our hut, or, as I preferred to believe, had been eaten during the day by a gecko, or better yet, a scorpion. Tom didn't. He tossed and turned from dusk to dawn, and in the morning looked very peaked. I was glad to see our boat show up as scheduled, and as we motored upriver I worried about what I would tell his parents if I let him die out here. He seemed a little better by the time we reached the Dzanga Sangha station that evening, and he was hungry — a good sign. As usual Allard's cook had a good meal waiting. We sat down to it with Allard and discussed Tom's malady Allard agreed that it might be malaria. But when he saw Tom drowning his meal in salt he smiled at us and remarked that sometimes animals have more sense than people have.

"What?" I said.

"Tom is suffering from salt depletion." Allard explained.

Tom looked at Allard, then back at his chicken, buried in salt, and replied. "Yeah, that must be it. I could have eaten a whole case of Pringles last night." Then he poured even more salt on his fowl, and ate it with relish.

CHAPTER TWENTY-FIVE

BILSA

*"The destruction of the earth's tropical rainforests is
a catastrophe second only to thermonuclear war."*
— Dr. Peter Raven, Director,
Missouri Botanical Garden

Out of sentiment, or maybe because I liked Mexican food, I still dined out at Casa de Lara once in a while by my lonesome. One evening there was a new hostess greeting customers. She was dark-haired, thin and spoke with an exotic accent. I loitered after the meal, talked to her, found out she was from Russia, and made a date with her. She stood me up. But I asked her out again, and the second time she was waiting at her door for me, all dolled-up. We went out to dinner, and she told me about herself, how she had wanted to get out of her country and come to America to make a good life for her and her son. She had done a lot of bribing to get a departure visa from Russia for herself, and was still trying to get her son out. Our date ended with a kiss on the cheek and a confession from her that she was already in love. However she said I was really nice and would be very popular in Russia.

This got me thinking, and after a couple of chats over tea in a cafe with my Russian friend I decided to make a call on Moscow to find my Lara — the heroine in the movie *Dr. Zhivago*. The third ICRN conference in England was coming up anyway, and it would be a simple matter to combine the two trips.

In preparation for the first stop on my itinerary I tracked down my long-lost adopted brother, Donny. He had learned to speak Russian as an interpreter when he was in the service, and I hoped to get some language lessons from him. Donny was living near Whitewater, Wisconsin, with his wife and three boys. He invited me to his home, and over a wonderful meal that his wife cooked Donny told me about the old days, when the Calhoun farm empire and baseball team had been in full glory. Later he told me how much he had loved his own trip to Russia a few years ago, but how he'd felt bad about his command of the language. People had thought he was from a town in Siberia because he spoke with an inflection.

"Poor guy," I reflected sarcastically. "He only learned to speak Russian, one of the most difficult languages in the world, well enough to be mistaken for a native from a rural part of the country."

Donny taught me a few words that I pronounced with great difficulty. He probably thought I was a dunce, and when it came to languages, I was. What little French I'd learned for my trip to the Central African Republic — a former French colony — had been woefully inadequate, and my Spanish, which should have been perfect by now, was embarrassingly flawed. My lack of progress this first evening prompted another visit just before I departed for Russia. During this visit Donny told me a lot of things I didn't know about our father, who had now been dead for over twenty years. It was also on this visit that Donny broke down in tears as he related, for the first time ever, exactly what had happened on that raw and ugly November day when Father died of a heart attack. How he had urged Dad to go out and work on the corn-bin that morning, despite the fact that Father had felt poorly.

In Moscow I hooked up with a men's' tour group and attended some of their receptions, to which marriage-minded Russian women were invited. This is how I met Alla. Alla was a handsome, intelligent and classy woman. She had divorced a husband who'd been second-in-command of a Soviet Union nuclear submarine, because he became an alcoholic after his mighty ship was decommissioned. The disintegration of the Soviet Empire had also cost Alla her high post as chief librarian at the Murmansk Public Library. Alla had one son, who lived fifty miles away with her mother. Alla wanted to marry an American and flee her country's hardships.

I was very attracted to Alla, and she seemed ecstatic to have found me. We spent eleven romantic days together in Moscow, walking Red Square, shopping for the decorative Russian Eggs that my sister Kathy wanted, going out to dinner, visiting museums and attending two incredible performances at the Bolshoi Theater. We took the Moscow Metropolitan Subway to all these places. That was sometimes the best part of our dates, for the subway tunnels were works of art. They had hanging chandeliers, stately support columns and sculpted reliefs, and were a hangout for minstrels who played tender melodies. More than once Alla and I embraced each other behind a column and kissed deeply as a saxophone player tenderly played *If It Takes Forever* or *Somewhere My Love.*

On my second-to-last day in Moscow I was invited to Alla's apartment for tea, and to meet her mother and son. It was such a blustery day that I could barely maintain my grip on the teacake, and roses I brought to the affair, and as I entered the dreary concrete apartment building where she lived I was thankful to be out of the wind and rain. I took a broken-down elevator to the third floor, stepped off, found her apartment and knocked. Alla opened the door with a big smile and bid me come in. In contrast to the starkness of her building, Alla's little apartment was warm and cozy. Every corner was neatly furnished with antique-looking cabinets and small coffee tables. The floor was covered with a beautiful rug that depicted a horse-drawn sleigh traveling through a winter landscape. The walls were tastefully papered, and in the center of the room was a dining table crowded with dishes of salami, ham, crackers, bread, fruit, salad, and cookies. Alla must have spent a month's salary to lay out such a spread.

She introduced me to her mother, and to her son, who was very shy at first. Then we sat down to our tea. Alla's son, unaccustomed to such grand banquets, stuffed himself, much to the pleasure of both his mother and grandmother. I sipped at my tea and tried to eat just enough to be polite. Afterward, I played ball with Alla's boy in the tiny bedroom while Alla and her mother cleaned up. Then it was time to go.

At the airport the next day Alla told me I had been approved by her mother and liked by her son, and that, yes, she would marry me. I got on the airplane thinking I had finally done it, I

had finally, finally found the woman for me. It had required flying halfway around the world and learning the rudiments of an
impossible language, but anything worth having…

Robin and his new girlfriend picked me up when I landed at
Heathrow. As we drove to his home near Peterbourgh we caught
up on each other's lives. In the last two years Robin had married
and divorced a stunningly beautiful woman, and subsequently
fallen in love with Vicki, a woman half his age. Vicki laughed and
said it was true. She joked that she had only been interested in his
money, but by the time she had found out he was going broke
because of the crash in real estate it was too late. She had become
addicted to his wit and Oxford charm. This was easy to believe,
for Robin was the quintessential Englishman — distinguished-
looking, articulate, world-traveled, unflappable, congenial, humorous and gallant.

The Kerns, Daniel and Matzumi, who represented the Japan
group at this meeting, were ensconced in Robin's castle-like stone
block home when we arrived from the airport. They had come
in a day earlier. They greeted me warmly, and we had a wonderful dinner amid the fifteenth-century tapestries, old family por-
traits, stuffed birds, suits of armor and shelves of rare books. Robin
told us this conference would be the last hurrah for the Rectory
because his real estate business had collapsed along with the British economy and he was going to have to sell the place for a
paltry half-million dollars to pay off his debts. He related this in
the matter-of-fact way that upper class Englishman always talked
about disaster. Then he entertained us with stories about the five
hundred-year old Rectory we were guests in: how the massive,
scarred oak table we ate on had been used as a bed for invalids
when the Black Death had terrorized England; how the cem-
etery of the adjoining church was filled with the graves of rectors
who had inhabited the rectory for centuries; and how ghosts
haunted some of the rooms upstairs.

After the meal he and Bernd, the Director of the Swedish
group, drank sherry and smoked up a storm while Eha, his wife,
Matzumi and Daniel, the leader of the German group, did dishes,
and Vicki and I played songs on the piano at the base of the grand
staircase. The night didn't conclude until we resumed our seats at
the dinner table for a strawberry creampuff desert, a glass of port,

and more conversation. We were all in a merry mood, happy to
be reunited, glutted with good food and liquor, and looking forward to the substantive talks that we were to begin, but not until
the morrow.

Bernd took charge the next day. We all summarized our operations for the last two years. Robin's UK fundraising had dipped
even lower than STR's. German and Japanese earnings were stag-
nant. Even Barnens Rengskog of Sweden was having trouble
getting donations. Bernd told us he thought the fat times were
over and that we would have to skin the cat another way. He
suggested we try to get our respective government aide agencies
to match our donations at a ratio of two or three to one, as he was
doing with Sweden's International Aide Agency. Then he gave
his usual tirade on how the big conservation groups were getting
all the money and wasting it on luxuries, while we were un-
tainted and would continue to be a shining beacon to those children who trusted so much in us.

I thought Bernd was too hard on the well-known conservation groups. Huge organizations like The Nature Conservancy
and World Wildlife Fund were working on a large scale and doing an enormous amount of good. I relied on their scientists'
research for a lot of information, and had always found their staff
people very helpful. It was TNC that had put me in touch with
Cliff Ross and the folks at ANCON in Panama, and WWF that
had provided me with the crucial support to do the video in
Africa. The large environmental organizations were weak in one
area, though, responding to the deluge of children's innocent and
naive questions about the rainforest. This is one reason they liked
schools and children to work through organizations like Cliff's
and mine. We were good at dealing with kids and classrooms. In
my case I handed over all student letters to an STR board member, Butch Beedle, whose middle school students, published *The
Tropical Tribune,* a newspaper written by and for young people.
Butch would divvy up the letters I sent him to his student staff,
who would read each and every letter, research the questions,
and answer them in the next issue of the paper, which was delivered to the classes that had written to us.

I told Bernd and the others about this, and Bernd nodded his
approval. I had come a long way in his estimation since our first

encounter in Costa Rica. He thought STR's ecology courses were a good idea too, and had been very impressed with my friends at Fundacion Jatun Sacha when he visited their reserve in Ecuador. FJS was a perfect match for Bernd. They managed their programs on a no-frills, shoestring budget. The staff spent most of their time working under tough conditions in the field, did almost all their travel to sites by public bus, and got things done. This is why Bernd continued to fund FJS's programs, and why our ICRN conference ended in a general agreement to keep purchasing land around Jatun Sacha and give FJS some help establishing a new reserve at Bilsa, in Western Ecuador.

After returning from the conference in England, I worked on getting a fiancée visa for Alla. While we waited for it to come through, Alla and I wrote and faxed one another. I told her more about Wisconsin, about the winters, the culture, the countryside and my family. She told me how she was looking forward to cross-country skiing with me in Governor Dodge Park, to learning English, to meeting my mother, to listening to me play the piano and to making a loving home for us. She also told me how excited her boy was getting about coming to the United States of America and living in a big house with a dog and a cat and a room all to himself.

"But do you have soccer?" she asked. "He loves to play soccer."

I faxed her back that we most certainly did, that there was a coed soccer league for children right in Dodgeville.

When the State Department notified me that Alla's visa had been approved I was primed and ready to start a new life. My work with STR was very rewarding, but now I was about to attain personal happiness as well, to enter into a lifelong relationship that would fulfill the needs that every man has. Alla's needs and her son's would be fulfilled too. I would be rescuing them from the chaos and ruin that had befallen their proud nation, providing a safe, comfortable home for them, and most importantly, giving Alla a husband's love, and her son a father's.

I called Alla. She answered, sounding funny. I told her the visa had been approved and was waiting for her at the American Embassy in Moscow. She didn't seem enthused. Then I told her I was going to buy her and her son plane tickets and send them to her by DHL courier.

She said, "Please don't, I can't come to Wisconsin and marry you."

That was that. I couldn't get any kind of an explanation out of her, and after she hung up I realized she could have been one of those women who would have accepted the tickets and cashed them in. I had been a better judge of character than that. Why, why had she changed her mind?

Completely deflated, I handed over the day to day management of STR to Rhonda, my secretary, dropped Cassandra at my mother's house, left Q, my cat, in Roland's care, and flew to Honduras. Honduras had proved the one place where our courses experienced continual problems. Every summer I received a complaint from one group or another about the vans breaking down or the food being bad or the dormitories being uncomfortable. None of these groups wanted me to discontinue the Honduran course; they just wanted me to correct the problems. So I decided to go down for a period of five weeks to consult with our partner there, Fundacion Prolansate, take some Spanish lessons and get away from my empty house in Dodgeville.

Part of the problem with Fundacion Prolansate was that its founder and president, Jeanette Kawas, had been assassinated in 1995 because someone hadn't liked her leading a protest against the destruction going on in Punta Sal National Park. No one ever found out who killed her, and the park was renamed after Jeannette, but Prolansate was rudderless without her for a while, and our courses, which she had worked hard with me to establish, had suffered as a consequence.

During my five weeks in Honduras I discussed general policy and finances with Rafael Sambula, the director of Prolansate, and went over the details of the coming year's courses with Miriam Molina, the environmental education coordinator. Miriam and Rafael did not get along very well — another reason our courses weren't running smoothly.

After one of my meetings with Miriam she asked me if I would loan her three thousand dollars so she and her husband could begin construction of their new house. She said she couldn't borrow the money from a bank because mortgage rates in Honduras were prohibitively high. I liked Miriam, and she had worked hard to make our courses a success, so I wrote her a personal check. I

was an easy touch this way. I had loaned my mother seven thousand dollars not long before so she could purchase a house trailer
for my sister Nancy to live in.

Most of my time in Honduras was spent in San Pedro Sula, it's
second largest city. I had a nice little apartment within walking
distance of the language school I attended every morning. One
day as I was walking home, a street hustler accosted me. He asked
if I wanted to buy some weed. I shook my head and kept walking. Then he asked if I wanted a girl.

I said, "No, Gracias."

At this point a pickup truck breezed through a stop sign at our
intersection and knocked over a bicyclist. The truck driver stopped
and got out to help the cyclist. While he was doing that the hustler looked around, saw that the coast was clear, and went to the
bicycle with the intention of making off with it while everyone
was distracted. I frustrated his purpose by grabbing hold of the
bicycle's frame at about the same time he did and "helping him"
put the bike in the bed of the truck. This we did as the driver
assisted the stricken cyclist into the cab of his truck to rush him
to the hospital.

Toward the end of that five-week stay I was involved in another street incident. I was driving back to my apartment in a car
I had rented for a trip to the Mayan ruins at Copan. It was late at
night and I got caught in traffic in the red-light district, a bad part
of town to be in after dark. There were three lanes of traffic, all
blocked by cabs dropping off or waiting for fares. I sat with my
window rolled up and doors locked, watching the pimps and
doormen work the street. One of these pimps saw me and was
walking toward my car when the lane to my right opened up. I
looked behind me, saw I was clear, and backed up a few feet so I
could swing around the cab in front of me and into the open
lane. When I again looked forward the pimp was limping in front
of my car as if I had run over his foot with my front tire while
backing up.

I didn't know whether to laugh or cry. His feigning looked
ridiculous and it was obvious that he was trying to shake me
down, but I knew that if I stopped to argue with him I would get
taken for every dollar I had. So I made a split-second decision to
scoot around him. When he saw this he gave up his limp, pulled

out the pistol hidden in his coat and ran to the side of the car. He pointed his gun straight at my head, while his friend in the cab that had been in front of me turned out into the open lane in an attempt to cut me off. I called the pimp's bluff and accelerated past him with such speed that I was also able to slip through the open lane before the cab could block the way. As I raced away I looked in the rearview mirror to see the pimp putting his pistol away with disgust.

I returned from Honduras the day after Q had died from what the vet's autopsy determined was kidney failure. Then my tearful mother informed me that Nancy had left the door open at mother's house and Cassandra had gotten out and run off. My place in Dodgeville was now emptier than ever, and I decided it was time to move on. I would have moved out of Dodgeville sooner but I hadn't wanted to disrupt STR business. The 888 toll-free number we now had was transferable though, and the post office assured me they would forward all mail, so I felt I could make a fresh start somewhere without losing touch with any of our member schools. I decided to relocate in Las Cruces, New Mexico, because Jeff and Mary were living next door in Demming, the climate was great, the nearby Organ Mountains were beautiful, and Juarez, Mexico was only forty-five minutes away.

Juarez was a typical border town in that it was dirty and corrupt, but I had visited it and liked it because I could practice Spanish there and immerse myself in its culture. It was also a lively place for a single man who liked dating Hispanic women.

So in July 1998, I walked out the door of my house in Dodgeville for the last time and took up residence in Las Cruces, bringing STR with me. After setting up a new office I joined Renee's, the best aerobic gym in town, and Varsity Club, a good place to lift weights. I made a lot of friends at these two gyms, and one at a ladies' bar in Juarez.

Ladies' bars are places where Mexican men go to drink and talk to the numerous women bartenders who sit across the counter from them on stools. They're pleasant places for a man to practice his Spanish. Lt. Colonel Johnny Virgin, who, I soon learned, was stationed at Fort Bliss in El Paso, came up to me in one of these bars and started a conversation. It wasn't long before he was driving me around town and showing me all his spots. His favorite was Valentino's, a classy nightclub that filled with women on Thursday nights, "Ladies' Night."

Over the next few months Colonel Virgin and I became friends, and went out to drink and pursue Latina women in tandem. Johnny was looking for wife number three. I told him I was still working on *numero uno*. One night Johnny told me about his second wife, a woman who had become more interested in winning the title of Mrs. North Carolina than in being Mrs. Virgin. When they divorced, the bird business they'd built up together was ruined. This is what really upset the Colonel. He had loved tropical birds every since he was thirteen, when his uncle had brought him a parrot from Columbia, and it killed him to lose the birds he had rescued from quarantine and set up in breeding pairs. I was sorry to hear about this, but not as sorry as I was about some of the bird businesses that I knew were operating undercover and still flourishing, the illicit ones that caught wild birds and dealt in rare and endangered species. Johnny knew about these outfits too, and deplored them as I did. He knew that wild birds were an important part of their environment. He also knew that they went crazy in captivity and made bad pets.

As 1998 came to a close I became too busy to hang out with Colonel Virgin very much. In an effort to boost course registrations I came up with a program called "Project Invite." This program would seek out some of the best biology, geography and Spanish teachers in the United States and send them to our sites for free in the summer of 2000, with the idea that they would return with a group of students to participate in our 2001 courses. I wrote several grant proposals to charitable institutions like the Turner Foundation asking for the hundred thousand dollars I needed to implement "Project Invite." The proposal stated that an investment of a hundred thousand dollars would fund fellowships for sixty teachers. If even half the teachers returned to our sites with students in 2001, about six hundred thousand dollars in earned income would be generated for ANCON, Fundacion Jatun Sacha, and Fundacion Prolansate — organizations on the front lines of tropical rainforest conversation, and very keen on hosting a greater number of STR groups. In addition to giving the above-mentioned foundations a big financial boost, "Project Invite" would introduce hundreds of students to the rainforest, an experience that would have a profound effect on many of them. My proposal included a copy of a fax I had received from a student who had taken our courses in the past:

Date: Fri, 12 Dec 97 12:42:44 CST
From: christina.mccain@tpwd.state.tx.us
To: saverft@mhtc.net

Hello! I just happened upon your web page the other day and decided to send a note. I went on two Save the Rainforest trips in a row several years ago. First to Belize, when you only offered Belize and Costa Rica, and the next year to the brand new Ecuador trip at Jatun Sacha. Those were the most incredible experiences of my life. I graduated from college a year ago, and am now applying for graduate programs in tropical forest ecology. The trips make a huge difference in the lives of the kids who go on them. You all probably already know that, but I just wanted to say it. I'm so glad you're still around and I see it's expanded a lot!

Just wanted to say thanks.

After sending out the proposals, I planned a trip to Panama and Ecuador to review the status of our current programs and prepare staff people for the increased number of groups they could expect in 2001. I left STR's office in the capable hands of Kimberly Smith, a very intelligent, beautiful and dynamic woman I'd met while working out at Renee's. She had been teaching for ten years, was wrapping up her Ph.D. in the uses of technology in public schools, had her own consulting business and spoke Spanish better than I. She wished me good luck on my trip. Then the forty-seven year old Lt. Colonel John M. Virgin, who had just married Mireya Alonso de Idez — a twenty-five year old Hispanic woman he met at Valentino's — picked me up and took me to El Paso's airport. Johnny Virgin it seemed was just as irresistible to the young ladies as was my debonair friend from England, Robin Jollife.

On the long flight to Quito, Ecuador I wrote the "One Hundred Roses" chapter of *Close Calls and Foolhardy Romances*. The plane touched down while I was putting the final touches on the last paragraph, and I cleared my head for the work I had come to do. Mike McColm met me outside the terminal after I cleared customs, and took me by cab to the hotel. Mike didn't have his own car; he relied on the many forms of public transportation Ecuador offered, thinking that as an environmentalist he should take advantage of them.

After I checked into the modest hotel where our groups stayed when they arrived in Ecuador, Mike and I took a seat by the fireplace in the lobby. We talked about "Project Invite," FJS's progress at Jatun Sacha, the reforestation project Mike hoped to undertake on a hundred and twenty thousand hectares of banana plantation land, and about Bilsa, where we were headed early the next morning. We also discussed FJS's management of the Guandera Reserve. This was the second reserve that FJS had, with our help, established. It protected one of the last remaining inter-Andean cloud forests, and an area of alpine *paramo* where spectacled bears roamed, from clearing by charcoal-makers and potato farmers.

I slept well that night, and in the morning we departed for Bilsa in a rented four-wheel drive truck driven by one of Mike's staff people. We drove out of Quito and down the western slope of the Andes until we reached the crossroads of Quinendae. From there it was a short drive to the turnoff that took us up to Bilsa, or within eight miles of Bilsa, for the road got so muddy that the truck could get no closer. Mike had anticipated this, and radioed the Bilsa station manager to have a couple of park rangers meet us with two mules at the little village of Chuvauycu, where the truck dropped us off and turned back for Quito.

We loaded up the mules and started on our long uphill walk. As we made our way through the mud, which was knee-deep at times, Mike told me how it got worse during the rainy season.

"In April," he said, "four-wheel drive trucks can only negotiate their way to within fifteen miles of the station, and the mud is so deep that the mules are up to their bellies in it."

"They can walk through mud that deep?" I asked.

"Sure," Mike answered, "but horses can't. We don't use them up here."

"How long does it take you to make the hike under those conditions?

"Eight hours for our rangers, ten hours for me, and we've had office people from Quito who just plain gave up and turned back."

"How long a walk will we have?" I asked

"This isn't too bad, four and a half hours I'd say. But it will be easier for your summer groups. By June the road is dried out and we can walk them to the station in a few hours and show them things along the way."

We hiked on, and Mike filled me in on Western Ecuador. "Only 3 percent of the forest remains here. Most of that is in the fifty thousand-hectare Mache Chindul Ecological Reserve that's supposed to be managed by the Ecuador's Park Service. But the government just dissolved the park service. It's just as well, the park service was inefficient and corrupt."

"So who's going to mind the store now?" I asked

"In theory the Ministry of Environment. But really it's the Provincial Land Title Office. The local Land Title people make a living from granting land claims, so they refuse to recognize the Mache Chindul Reserve. They've been giving out possession rights to settlers. That's why the reserve is peppered with small farms. Right now most of these farms are still 90 percent forested."

"How does your work at Bilsa fit into this?" I questioned.

"Well," Mike explained, "in a worst case scenario the Mache Chindul Reserve is completely deforested by settlers and loggers, and our thirty-two hundred hectares becomes the last tiny island of Western Ecuadorian forest left on the planet. In a best case scenario our community outreach program at Bilsa demonstrates to the farmers in Mache Chindul that it's in their best interest to leave most of the forest on their homesteads intact."

"How will your programs do that?"

"By supplying farmers with an alternative, sustainable way to make a better living. Right now they subsist on corn, beans and a few other vegetables, and raise pigs that they can walk out of the reserve and sell for cash. We want to distribute saplings of fruit and nut trees to them, which in a few years will provide the farmers enough nutritious food to feed their families and enough surplus to sell in markets. We'll encourage them to plant valuable hardwoods like Mahogany, Tangare, and Cedro, too. In twenty or thirty years those trees will be mature enough to harvest for timber. Planting them is sort of like putting money in an IRA account."

Mike continued educating me, growing more enthusiastic as he revealed what a Garden of Eden Bilsa was. He told me more about the ninety species of fruit and nut trees of the region, how some produced a softball-sized fruit so concentrated that it could make fifty glasses of juice. How others had protein-rich seeds that taste like fish, how the *Pourima cecropifolia* tree hung with clusters of purple, peach-flavored "grapes," and how the prolific fruit of the cacao Blanca, when fried, tasted like sunflower seeds.

Then he told me more about the Bilsa forest. There were over fifteen hundred species of vascular plants and eighty species of trees per hectare. There were jaguars, giant anteaters, mantled howler monkeys, five-foot river otters that he had seen eating bananas at the station, the endemic Choco toucan, banded ground-cuckoos, and long-wattled umbrella birds that were found nowhere else in breeding numbers. In addition there were numerous species of reptiles, amphibians and insects. All this life inhabited steep, fog-shrouded ridges, and deep ravines drained by numerous streams.

Mike's narrative tailed off when we ran out of light about three miles from the station. The road was muddier, steeper and more difficult to pick our way along by the light of our hand lamps and we had to concentrate on our walking. Mike stepped in a two-foot hole and nearly broke his leg. I fell behind our caravan when I had a sudden attack of diarrhea and had to make a pit stop. I didn't catch up to my guides until I had made a wrong turn in the dark, started down a suspiciously steep hill, retraced my steps back to the right road and double-timed it for ten minutes. By the time we reached Bilsa station I was exhausted, and wondering how Mike and the rest of his people could make the fifteen-mile trip in April when the mud was twice as bad.

Soraya, Chris, Carlos, and Gladys greeted us. Gladys — Mike's long-haired Quichua wife — and Soraya had organized a women's cooperative for the purpose of disseminating information on health, nutrition and sanitation, and marketing crafts that the locals made from palm hemp. Chris, a volunteer worker from the

states, co-managed the station with Carlos, who had grown up in
the area and had played a crucial role in FJS'S purchase of the
thirty-two hundred hectares of Bilsa. We all sat down to a good
hot meal after which I retired for the evening.

The next day Mike took me on a hike into the Bilsa Reserve.
It had the classic look of a rainforest. The tree ferns I had first
encountered in El Junque were abundant. There were two-hun-
dred-foot tall Guyacan trees whose wood was so dense and du-
rable that houses made from it lasted for centuries. There were
orchids and bromeliads hanging from every branch, vines dan-
gling down from treetops, and waterfalls everywhere. Mike and I
sat at the foot of one of these waterfalls and had our lunch.

"The flora and fauna here are internationally renowned for
both their diversity and rarity," Mike explained. "Norman Myers,
the British botanist, has included this forest on his "hotspot" list as
one of the ten habitats in the world that is being lost and needs to
be saved."

"Isn't this where Gentry and Dodson went down in a plane
while doing an aerial survey of the forest?" I asked.

"Yes," said Mike, "the forests of Western Ecuador were going
so fast that they felt they had to do a rapid assessment of what was
here. It cost them their lives. We've named our main meeting hall
at the station after them."

"Is anyone else besides FJS working in this region?"

"Not really, Fundacion Natura had a reforestation project going for a while but it fizzled."

"Why?" I inquired.

"Natura staff people like their office in Quito. They didn't
come out in the field very often, and you have to be here on the
ground to accomplish anything."

"What about The Nature Conservancy?"

"They've been supporting work in other parts of Ecuador, but
they are aware of the importance of the forest here. Conservation
International, World Parks Endowment and the Wheeden Foundation have gotten involved. They donated the money that we
bought the thirty-two hundred hectares with."

"How are you funding your community outreach?"

"Your Swedish friends and The Dutch International Union
for the Conservation of Nature gave us the money that paid for

the construction of the station and is funding our current programs."

"Well, I'm sold on this place," I said. "We'll start bringing our
groups here next year. In the meantime we'll do some fundraising
to help you expand the reserve."

"How much do you think you can raise for us?"

"Maybe twenty thousand dollars in the next school year. I
wish it could be more."

"I do too," Mike rejoined. "I calculate we're going to need
around four hundred thousand to finish up the land purchases
we need to make."

"You know," I said thoughtfully, "Cliff Ross from the Earth's
Birthday Project called me a month ago and asked if I knew of
any really good projects he could support. He raises about half a
million dollars each year for The Nature Conservancy's "Adopt
an Acre" program. I think I can interest him in raising money for
you, on the condition that TNC approves of your plan of action."

"That would be fantastic! We'd like to buy some of the adjoining properties before the logging companies move in."

"What is land going for here?"

"About a hundred and twenty dollars per hectare. That comes
out to fifty dollars an acre, and includes the titling fee, which we
still owe on about two thousand hectares that we only have the
possession rights to."

"That's a bargain," I said, and offered him one of the low-fat
raspberry fruit and grain cereal bars I had brought down with
me from the states.

"Man, these are good!" he exclaimed.

The next day Carlos, who knew Bilsa better than anyone else,
guided Mike and me on a hike through another part of the reserve. Carlos spotted golden frogs, coaxed the big soldier leaf-
cutter ants from their nests for us to observe, and took us to one
of the highest ridges in the reserve, where we were treated to a
magnificent view. On the way back to the station Carlos cautioned me to be careful of the spiny palm tree that was next to
the trail. I stopped to regard its thin, sharp, protective thorns, and
broke off the tip of a spine to use as a toothpick. As I cleaned my
teeth with the hard and handsome black spine it occurred to me
that we could pay the local people a very good wage to harvest

these spines, which STR would sell in the states as "Save the Rainforest Deluxe Toothpicks and Party Skewers."

Mike liked the idea, and Soraya loved it. That night she and I sat down to work out the details. In addition to harvesting the spines her contractors would need to pinch off the sharp tips and package them in the small envelopes I would provide. I told her we only needed a hundred thousand spines to start off with. After we established ourselves in the market place we would need millions. When Soraya and I finished our work we joined the rest of the camp staff in its celebration of the beginning of Carnaval, Latin America's Mardi Gras-like three-day holiday.

"You better watch out during Carnaval," warned Soraya. "People will be throwing buckets of water at each other and shooting at everyone with big homemade squirt rifles for the next two days."

I shared a big bottle of pilsner beer with her and told her I would.

I went to bed soon after, listened to the lullaby sounds of the forest that surrounded us, and fell quite to sleep. I was wakened at about 5:00 A.M. by a cute little rainforest rodent that had taken up residence in the station building and was inspecting my pack for goodies. It had discovered a raspberry bar and was eating it with as much pleasure as Mike had eaten his the day before.

I couldn't get back to sleep so I went for a short walk, and as dawn slowly broke over the foggy forest a troop of howler monkeys began to roar in the distance. Their wild calls gave me the same feeling of being in an ancient and pristine place as had the elephant trumpeting in Africa and the lonely howling of the wolves in Alaska.

There were twelve troops of howler monkeys in Bilsa, Mike had told me, and their vocalizations were territorial in nature. The howlers didn't write down their property rights on bits of paper or establish homestead claims by "improving the land." They simply roamed the treetops as they have for millions of years, searching for edible fruits and leaves, and heckling their neighbors when they got too close on foggy mornings like this one.

After breakfast Mike and I set off down the mountain to Chuvauycu, where we would catch the big open-bed cargo truck that transported the locals to Quinendae. On our way out of the reserve Mike showed me where he and his staff had planted some of their quarter-million fruit, nut and timber seedlings over the last three years in an effort to reforest the logged-over areas of Bilsa's buffer zone. He showed me how they had interspersed Cedro, a timber species, with Inga, the fruit tree that produces the fishy-tasting seeds and also fixes nitrogen in the soil, thereby replenishing it so the Cedro trees would grow better. Then he pointed out where he wanted to plant his twelve thousand mahogany seedlings.

"We have to space the mahogany twelve meters apart and plant vegetation between them to prevent infestation by the *Hysphlya* butterfly larva that eat the meristem of young mahogany and kill them," Mike informed me.

"When your mahogany mature you'll be able to harvest some of them and have plenty of money for your programs," I speculated.

Mike smiled. "We've made a plan for a sustainable forestry program that would rotate harvests of designated plots once every hundred and twenty years. We hope to be supporting ourselves long before that through the sale of the produce from our fruit and nut trees. They should be maturing in a couple more years. Until then we're going to need your help."

"We'll do what we can," I assured him, and we continued on our way.

Along the road we passed a couple of schools that I hadn't seen when we'd come up in the dark. They were no more than small wood shacks with tin roofs, but they both had some open pasture around them that the children had reforested with seedlings provided by Bilsa. Mike was so enthusiastic about showing me how these trees had grown that at the second school he stepped in a deep hole in the road. He looked down at his leg that was thigh-high in water and said, "That's the same hole I stepped in on the way up."

At this moment Mike reminded me a little bit of my old friend Steve when a joke had been played on him. I helped him out of the hole and we reached Chuvauycu two hours later. But the truck was not there; it was another six miles down the road, which had become more impassable because of the heavy rain that had fallen the night before. We walked that last six miles in record time, under a hot sun that had come out from behind the clouds.

The truck was waiting for us at the end of our hike, its back end loaded with ten standing passengers dressed in their Sunday best for a visit to Quinendae. Our ranger escort untied our gear from the mules and threw it up into the truck. Then Mike and I climbed aboard. The driver rose off the stump he was sitting on, walked over to the truck and invited Mike and me to drink from his bottle. I was going to turn the offer down but then I remembered it was Carnaval. So I took a sip of his rotgut. So did Mike.

After that the driver got in the cab and we started down the bumpy road. I felt exhilarated by the wind in my face as we jolted along, holding onto the sides of the truck so I wouldn't fall over. I felt that we were still in frontier country, and perhaps we had gotten to Bilsa in time. I felt that I could talk Cliff Ross, who had, like my dear old friend Greg, once been my rival, into donating the money needed to expand the park. I felt we would be able to sell so many Bilsa toothpicks that the local farmers would forget about cutting down trees and raising pigs, and concentrate on harvesting the endless supply of spines. I felt that Mike's beloved trees would grow fast in the tropical climate, and provide a bountiful future for the local population.

But who was to say? There were still the logging companies that bribed government officials, still the grinding poverty and 60 percent unemployment that drove people to sell timber rights on their homesteads, still the ignorance, still the schools with teachers who weren't paid and had to rely on the charity of the impecunious parents whose children they taught, still the lack of will on the part of Ecuadorian politicians to advocate social and environmental reforms.

I looked back toward the Bilsa Reserve one last time, wondering how much forest we would save. Then I had other things to worry about for it *was* Carnaval, and we were turning onto the paved highway lined with little farms, and I was reminded by the old man standing next to me that I had better be ready to duck, or some child, in the spirit of Carnaval, was going to douse me in the face with a bucket of water as we passed him, or her, on our way to Quinendae.

Bilsa Station, Western Ecuador

POSTSCRIPT

Two months after my visit to Bilsa I returned with Cliff Ross, director of The Earth's Birthday Project. He agreed to raise funds to save the precious forest there; however, deforestation in other places continues at a rampant rate. Unless something monumental is done, tropical forests and the myriad life forms they harbor will be all but gone by 2050. That is why I think the United States should institute a 'One Penny Per Gallon Earthsaver Tax' on gasoline. The Earthsaver monies would be used to preserve great tracts of existing rainforests and to reforest one billion acres of land in tropical countries. These forests will help keep global warming in check by absorbing much of the carbon dioxide we put into the atmosphere when we drive our automobiles. Many carbon emitting power utilities already do this—give funds to protect blocks of tropical forests as a way to compensate for the pollution they are causing. The Earthsaver tax would generate far more revenue, and would provide enough yearly income to save rainforests on a massive scale. It would also reflect the true end cost of burning carbon compounds that have been built up and stored in the earth's crust for millions of years. I urge all Americans to support the idea.

Individuals concerned about rainforests are welcome to become supporting members of SAVE THE RAINFOREST, INC. Members receive a newsletter three times a year that includes information on trips that we sponsor to the rainforests we are saving. Membership is $25.00. Checks may be sent to:

Save the Rainforest Inc.
P.O. Box 1627
Las Cruces, NM 88004

Bruce Calhoun earned a Bachelor of Science degree in biology at the University of Wisconsin, La Crosse, and earned another, in general science, at the University of Wisconsin, Madison. He taught marine biology for a year at San Juan School, in Puerto Rico, and then taught science at Dodgeville High School, in Dodgeville, Wisconsin for ten years. Calhoun also worked as a naturalist for the Wisconsin Department of Natural Resources for three summers, and spent a fourth as a research diving assistant at the Australian Institute of Marine Science.

In 1988 he founded Save the Rainforest, Inc., a teacher–student organization dedicated to promoting education and conservation of the world's tropical rainforests. Currently, Mr. Calhoun serves as its president, in which capacity he speaks at international conferences, consults with conservation groups in the tropics and produces educational videos and slide shows. He also conducts workshops and overseeing a travel–education program that sends hundreds of enthusiastic participants to Latin America each summer.